KIMMAGE MANOR

Patrick J. Ryan CSSp

Kimmage Manor

100 YEARS OF SERVICE TO MISSION

the columba press

First published in 2011 by
the columba press
55A Spruce Avenue, Stillorgan Industrial Park,
Blackrock, Co Dublin

Cover by Emer O Boyle
Origination by The Columba Press
Printed by Gemini International Limited

ISBN 978 1 85607 755 2

Contents

ACKNOWLEDGEMENTS

The writing of the story of Holy Ghost Missionary College, Kimmage Manor, arose out of the December 2010 deliberations of the organising committee for the celebrations in 2011 of the centenary of the involvement of the Spiritan (Holy Ghost) Congregation in Kimmage. The work effectively began two months later when I took up residence in the old novitiate where some of the earliest Spiritans in Kimmage lived. Here I had the opportunity of getting to know the old buildings at close quarters, examining them in detail, and imagining what life must have been like here one hundred years ago.

I also had the invaluable experience of being in close contact with the large community of Spiritans – some in active ministry, some retired and some sick – in the various houses that make up the Kimmage campus. They were immensely supportive, encouraging and forthcoming with endless nuggets of information about life in Kimmage in their own era. Their ages range from just under fifty to just over a hundred, so their experiences cover a wide spectrum. Many valuable insights were gained from formal interviews, casual conversations, written memoirs, memos and notes which were graciously proffered and received. Among those who shared their memories and insights were some who had studied in Kimmage, then decided this way of life was not for them but have kept up contact over many years.

The archives of the Irish Spiritan Province proved to be a veritable mine of information and documentation on the history of Kimmage, far more than could be handled in such a short time. For some historians in the future it will prove a fruitful field of labour. I wish to thank the Provincial Team and their staff for their unfailing help at all times; sincere thanks to Brother Ignatius Curry for directing me to some of the richest sources of our history. At very short notice, Joe Sheehan, the Kimmage librarian, was frequently able to provide me with whatever reference work I needed.

Seán Farragher of Blackrock College was a constant source of inspiration and information with his all-embracing knowledge of the Irish Spiritan Province and its personnel with all their virtues and foibles. His writings on Bishop Joseph Shanahan and Père Jules Leman were especially informative on the early days of the Irish Province.

I am deeply grateful to Joe Carroll, who at very short notice, read the script and made invaluable suggestions as to the organisation and editing of the text. I am particularly indebted to confrères Mick Reynolds, Tony Geoghegan, John B. Doyle and Pat Palmer who read all or portions of the text, pointed out omissions and made corrections and amendments.

I owe a special thanks to Dolorés Stewart and Pat McGlynn for typing the text from my handwriting, which at times I have difficulty in reading myself. The remarkable speed, with which they accomplished the task, astonished this two-finger typist.

I owe a continuing debt of gratitude to the Province's Communications Manager, Peter O'Mahony, who has borne the brunt of the work of correcting, editing and preparing the final draft for publication. He has also been an immense source of encouragement.

There were times when confrères asked if I had written about so and so or such and such in Kimmage community. I declined because communities like individuals are entitled to their privacy and not every experience can - or ought to - be made public.

ABBREVIATIONS

BCM	Minutes of Building Committee Meetings
BG	*Bulletin Général*. Bulletin de la Congregation
GTAN	*Go Teach All Nations*, edited by Enda Watters CSSp.
IPA	Irish Provincial Archives of the Congregation of the Holy Spirit
IPN	Irish Provincial Newsletter
ISR	Irish Spiritans Remembered, by Seán P. Farragher CSSp
KDSC	Kimmage Development Studies Centre
MA	*Missionary Annals*
PB	Provincial Bulletin of the Irish Province
Pro. Co.	Minutes of the Provincial Council of the Irish Province

FOREWORD

Brian Starken
Provincial

This centenary commemoration of the story of Kimmage Manor sets out to chronicle events as gleaned from Spiritan (Holy Ghost) Provincial Archives, from the memories and memoirs of Spiritans alive and dead, and from various writings over the years.

Its main aim is to try to tell as faithfully as possible how Holy Ghost Missionary College, Kimmage Manor came to be, and how it progressed through the course of the twentieth century to become one of the leading missionary colleges in Ireland. It outlines the slow beginnings, the rapid rise over forty or fifty years and then the more rapid decline to the point where at the time of writing there is only one Irish Spiritan student in formation.

An attempt has been made through the use of archives and personal memories to paint a picture, however incomplete, of what life was like on the Kimmage campus during the various phases of its development. This is set in a very general way in the context of the Irish missionary movement since the middle of the nineteenth century.

Just as historical commemoration plays an important role in national life, so too does it play a role in the lives of Irish Spiritans. Remembering is an important feature of our lives and of our Christian faith. The identity of Irish Spiritans for the past hundred years has been intimately connected with Kimmage. Prior to that it was connected to Spiritan colleges and juniorates in Ireland and houses of formation in France. Our present centenary commemoration marks our identity at this particular time. The main focus then of the book is on what happened and, to a lesser extent, why. It makes no pretence at being a critical history of Kimmage Manor; it is more a tour guide through one hundred years of how young men were prepared for mission. Neither is it in any way a history of the overseas missions of the Irish Spiritan Province. At a later time it will be possible for a person more removed from the events to do an analysis and a more critical history of the period. Too many of the makers of our Irish Spiritan history are still alive to allow for a more candid analysis of their contributions.

The oldest living Irish Spiritan, Fr Tim O'Driscoll, was born the year before the Congregation bought Kimmage Manor, was a novice in Kimmage in 1929-30, and was ordained in Kimmage in 1938, seeing its rapid rise and more dramatic decline. Others who are still alive were in Kimmage in the late thirties and early forties and all the years in between. Thomas Ohle, a parishioner in Kimmage parish, who was born on 3 September 1911, the day on which the first solemn High Mass was celebrated in Kimmage, still attends Sunday Mass in Kimmage parish church and remembers when most of the area from Mount Argus to the foothills of the Dublin Mountains was open country. That explains why so much of the narrative is descriptive rather than analytical.

INTRODUCTION

Buying the property called Kimmage Manor was remote from the thoughts of Fr John T. Murphy as he set out from Dublin on a cold February day in 1911. Fr Murphy, the Provincial of the Spiritan (Holy Ghost) congregation in Ireland, had been hastily dispatched to Paris, where the Mother House of the congregation was. His task was to seek permission from a reluctant Superior General to buy Dunfillan House, Rathgar, as a novitiate and house of studies. Archbishop William Walsh of Dublin had granted the Spiritans permission to buy the property, but then the Mother House in Paris refused. At a meeting with the Superior General, Mgr Alexander Le Roy, and with his Council, Fr Murphy's persuasive powers won the day. He sailed back to Ireland a happy man, only to be told on arrival that Dunfillan House had just been sold!

As luck would have it a number of other properties came on the market at that time. Using the permissions he had already acquired, Fr Murphy and his Council quickly settled on Kimmage Manor. As it turned out, this was a more suitable property than Dunfillan House: the location was ideal, just four miles from the new university in Earlsfort Terrace, where the students would study, and a tram service came to Terenure, the nearest village, a mere mile away while the house, set in beautifully wooded surroundings, provided the right atmosphere for the prayer and study requirements of a novitiate.

This house had a history stretching far beyond that of the Spiritans, who were founded in 1703. In early Norman times Kimmage began to appear in documents as Cammuch, Kamiuche and Camage. The latter name was still used in deeds of conveyance in 1911.[1] These names are variations of the old Irish name *Cam Uisce* which usually refers to a bend on a river or a winding stream – in this case of the river Poddle, the watercourse of the ancient city of Dublin.

---

1. IPA, Kimmage Manor, Box 1, File 10

The first Norman to hold these lands was Oliver the Goldsmith. They passed in quick succession to Audeon de Brun, and from him to Hugh de Barnewall. They remained the property of the Barnewalls until they were dispossessed by the Cromwellians in 1652, at which time there was a castle on the lands.

With the restoration of the monarchy in 1660 Richard Talbot, later Earl of Tyrconnell and Lord Lieutenant of Ireland, was granted the lands of Terenure and Kimmage. Eleven years later, Major Joseph Deane purchased these lands from Richard Talbot and they remained in the hands of the Deane family until 1761. Joseph Deane converted the castle in Terenure into a mansion which became known as 'Terenure House'.

Robert Shaw, Accountant General of the Post Office, a descendent of a Williamite officer who had settled in Kilkenny, leased Terenure House from the Deane family in 1785. Then four years later Abraham Wilkinson from Harold's Cross bought nearly all the Deane property in Terenure and Kimmage. A short time later he also purchased nearby Bushy Park House. Wilkinson's only child, Maria, married Robert Shaw Jr, in 1796. Bushy Park House and most of the lands of Terenure and Kimmage were part of her dowry. Thus began the Shaw connection with Kimmage. After their marriage Robert and Maria went to live in Bushy Park House which remained the Shaw family home until 1953.

Robert Shaw Jr had a distinguished career and when George IV visited Ireland in 1822, he was created a baronet. When he died in 1849 his title passed to his eldest son, also Robert. The younger Sir Robert never married and, when he died in 1869, his younger brother Frederick inherited the title. Sir Frederick is the only member of the family associated with Kimmage House having lived there from 1829. The leaseholder was the Revd John Exshaw, whose interest in the lease was bought by Sir Frederick, thus becoming a tenant to Sir Robert.

Sir Frederick studied at Trinity College and Oxford. At the age of 31 he became Recorder of Dublin, a position he held for 46 years. The Recorder was a barrister or solicitor of 10 years standing who served as a part-time, Crown Court judge with the municipality. Contrary to what many people believe, this office was not hereditary and Sir Frederick was the only member of the Shaw family to hold the office. In 1819 Sir Frederick married Thomasina Emily Jocelyn, daughter of George Jocelyn and granddaughter of the first Earl of Roden, founder of the Orange Order.

Already there were several buildings on the property occupied by what is now called the 'Manor House'. In the deed of conveyance it is stated that there was a 'Mansion House' with gardens there. Within two years it had been remodelled until it acquired its unique Tudor revival style with triangular gables, spiral turrets and tall chimneys. Different building techniques and different styles are evident in several features of the building which have been retained from the eighteenth century. The end result was a beautiful building with an Elizabethan look.[2] The architects who undertook the enterprise of renovation and extending the building were Richard Morrison and his son William.

Here in this beautiful house in a rural setting Frederick Shaw lived until his death in 1876. On his death, his eldest son, Robert became 4th Baronet. He moved to Bushy Park House and leased Kimmage House and lands to various tenants until finally, in 1898, it came into the hands of William Clayton and his wife, Mary Ida, and their three sons. One son, the architect William Geraty Clayton, is reputed to have added the bay window on the south elevation. During the tenancy of the Claytons the house became known as 'Kimmage Manor'. However, it never was a manor in any administrative or geographical sense.

Of special interest to Spiritans is Lady Flora Shaw, Sir Frederick's granddaughter. In her youth she came summer after summer to spend her holidays in Kimmage. Her father, Major General George Shaw, was based in London for most of his military career. Kimmage must have been an exciting change from the drab and dreary surroundings of Woolwich Arsenal where they lived. Flora began a career in journalism at the age of 34, eventually becoming Colonial Editor of *The (London) Times*. She travelled widely and earned a reputation as a balanced political commentator. It was she suggested the name Nigeria for the group of territories functioning under the cumbersome title of

---

2. Hugh O'Reilly, *The Old House, Tomorrow's Labourers*, 1954

the 'Royal Niger Company Territories', in an essay that appeared in *The Times* on 8 January 1897. In 1902 she married Sir Frederick Lugard, the first Governor General of Nigeria. In this newly named state, large numbers of Spiritans educated and trained in 'Kimmage Manor' would work as missionaries through several decades.

The original entrance to Kimmage House was through a long serpentine avenue which began almost opposite Laurel Lodge on Terenure Road West and corresponds approximately to today's Greenlea Road which was then known as Green Lanes. A later entrance came from Fortfield Road. The road approached the house from the south side and then came round to the main entrance where there was a roundabout. On this road there were three family cottages for workers at Kimmage House. Sometime before his death in 1876 Sir Frederick Shaw opened a new entrance from the newly constructed Whitehall Road, which became known locally as the Recorder's Road (*Bóthar an Racardair* still appears in the signage today) or, more popularly, 'The Milk Run' – from the number of milk carts from the surrounding farms using it to supply milk to the city.

Just inside the new entrance there was a gate lodge which in later times housed the ploughman and his family. The beautiful entrance in cut limestone had a letterbox for Sir Frederick. As one approached the buildings through a tree-lined avenue from Whitehall Road there was a walled garden with two large greenhouses on the site of the present walled garden but more extensive. Sadly, the entrance, letterbox and avenue have all disappeared.

The fields next to Whitehall Road were beautifully laid out like parklands with Spanish and Irish oak trees and a picturesque summerhouse. Where Kimmage parish church now stands was a cow-paddock completely secluded from the front of the house by a railing, a row of ornamental shrubs and trees. To the right and to the rear of the church stood the old farmyard complete with cow-byre, stables, forge workshop and barns.

It was this idyllic rural mansion with 69 acres of land that the Spiritans purchased in 1911 as a training centre for missionaries and which would go on to play such a central part in the mission of the Province. The story of how this expanded to become headquarters of the Irish Spiritans and the place of the spiritual and missionary formation of over a thousand students who passed through its halls has many twists and turns. The reader may find it helpful if we start by a sketch of the state of the Catholic Church in Ireland in the second half of the nineteenth century and the drive to find Irish vocations for the foreign missions.

CHAPTER ONE

An Irish Foundation

For most of the first half of the nineteenth century there was no
indigenous missionary movement in Ireland such as there was
in France. Indeed neither the old Holy Spirit Congregation
founded by Claude Poullart des Places in 1703, nor the
Congregation of the Holy Heart of Mary founded by Francis
Libermann in 1841 had any plans to extend the movement outside of their native France. Both movements were strictly French
in character. When Francis Libermann made tentative moves to
seek vocations from Ireland it was a matter of expediency.
Restrictions on French missionaries in the British colonies made
essential the introduction of missionaries who were British subjects if the missions were to be maintained. As early as 1842 the
French governor of Mauritius had vetoed the arrival of any further French priests on the island. To cope with this new situation Libermann initiated inquiries as to how best he might find
British subjects. He hoped to contact someone in England or
Ireland who might start a work similar to his own for the emanc-
ipation of slaves in the British colonies.

At this juncture Libermann had contact with Fr John Hand
who was preparing to launch a seminary in Dublin to train
priests mainly for the Irish of the diaspora. Libermann hoped to
interest Fr Hand in supplying him with suitable students who
would be willing to join his society and work for the blacks. The
response was poor. Fr Hand found the request a difficult one
because as Libermann wrote: 'The Irish are not generous enough
to renounce everything to the extent that is necessary for our
vocation'.[1]

Following the merger of the Congregation of the Holy Spirit
and the Society of the Holy Heart of Mary in 1848, Libermann
came to reside at what is now Rue Lhomond, almost across the
street from the Irish College in Paris. The Irish College had just
lost its very able director, Dr David Moriarty, who had been recalled to take over as rector of All Hallows in 1846. Before

---

1. Seán Farragher, *Père Leman, Educator and Missionary 1826-1880*, pp 86-87

leaving for Ireland, Dr Moriarty had visited Libermann at La Neuville and was favourably impressed by both the man and his institute. Without any establishment of his own society in England or Ireland, Libermann had given up hope of recruits from either country but the contacts he had established would eventually bear fruit.

When Francis Libermann died on 2 February 1852, he was succeeded by Fr Ignatius Schwindenhammer who almost immediately got down to the business of recruiting Irish personnel. Towards the end of May 1853 he was in contact with Dr Moriarty with requests for personnel on behalf of Bishop Collier of Mauritius and on behalf of Bishop Aloysius Kobes of the Gambia. Schwindenhammer was advised to approach Archbishop Paul Cullen of Dublin who was then in Paris en route from Rome. The immediate result was a number of recruits from Fr Thomas Bennett O Carm, who conducted a school in Aungier Street, Dublin. One of these students, Thomas Bracken, was to be the first fruit of the Irish foundation, the first Irish Spiritan. The long-term results of the contacts with Archbishop Cullen and other members of the Irish hierarchy and a reconnaissance trip to Ireland by Fr Louis Holley, was the decision by Fr Schwindenhammer and his Council to found an Irish house with Fr Jules Leman as founder.

Fr Leman, accompanied by Fr Jerome Schwindenhammer, brother of Fr Ignatius, Fr Louis Holley, Brother Philip and a novice, Brother Crescentius, arrived in Dublin on 28 October 1859. It was the twentieth anniversary of Libermann's decision to associate himself with the work of the evangelisation of the black race. They were well received by the Carmelite community in Whitefriar Street and on the following day went to see Archbishop Cullen. Shortly afterwards they visited Bishop David Moriarty in Kerry.

Almost immediately the four Spiritans set up a community in Blanchardstown. Their original intention had been to recruit candidates for the Congregation who were already as near as possible to ordination. They were soon to find out that the nearer these candidates were to the priesthood the less chance there was that they would opt for the religious missionary way of life. The candidates who presented themselves at Blanchardstown were all pursuing secondary studies at a senior level and on the whole were judged to be of a poor academic standard. As a result of these experiences Fr Leman made a plea for the establishment of a Juniorate in Ireland with a view to providing candidates with a coherent and satisfactory level of academic training. The numbers at Blanchardstown began to grow and by January 1860 there was insufficient room.

In the summer of 1860 the community transferred to Blackrock. Although it was Fr Jules Leman who made the plea, he realised that a Juniorate would need to be subsidised from France as there was no hope that the necessary funds could be raised in Ireland. The Spiritans had already given an undertaking that they would not seek to raise funds in the Diocese of Dublin and there was no prospect of fund-raising throughout the rest of the country where they were entirely unknown and where there was little interest in evangelising Africans. With the approval of the Mother House, a Junior Scholasticate was established at Blackrock on 21 June 1860 with the aim of getting volunteers for the salvation of the abandoned souls of the English-speaking missions, primarily in Africa. A little over a year later a brothers' novitiate was also opened in Blackrock. As a means to get resources to finance these works, a college had been opened at Blackrock in the autumn of 1860. It began with 34 boarders and 15 Junior Scholastics. The correspondence of the time regrets that scholastics were not as numerous as might be expected.[2]

This was to be the pattern for a whole century with the boarders far outnumbering the scholastics. The brothers' novitiate opened in 1861 with six postulants. In the summer of 1864 the Spiritans accepted the invitation of Mr Gustave Thiebaut (a Frenchman who had lived in Scotland and who had come to Ireland to care for the property bought some years earlier by his brother) to undertake the training of priests for the Scotch Mission at Rockwell in Co. Tipperary. This arrangement lasted until 1874. In the meantime the Archbishop of Cashel allowed lay pupils to become boarders and in 1865 another junior scholasticate was opened in Rockwell; in 1870 this was moved to the Lake House also known as St Joseph's.

---

2. Farragher, *op cit*, Chap 4, *passim*

The junior scholastics from Blackrock and Rockwell as well as some boarders who opted to join the congregation were sent to France for their studies for the priesthood and for their novitiate. At that time the novitiate year followed ordination thereby giving an opportunity to provide spiritual and pastoral training to people who were more mature. This was changed in 1892 with the Roman decree, *Auctis*, which required that ordination be postponed until after perpetual vows or at least until three years after first vows. The senior house of studies and novitiate was at Chevilly in the southern Paris suburbs. During the Franco-Prussian War of 1870-1871, Chevilly was turned into a battlefield and the senior scholasticate was transferred to Langonnet in Brittany until Chevilly was rebuilt. It was to this remote location that the first Irish clerical students and postulant brothers had been sent. When Chevilly became overcrowded in 1899, part of the student body was again sent to Langonnet. Already in 1886 it was decided to open a separate novitiate at Orly, another suburb of Paris. It was here that many Irish Spiritans did their year of novitiate.

The success of the Spiritans in the area of secondary education was enormous. Their success in recruiting candidates for religious missionary life was less spectacular.

Throughout the second half of the nineteenth century there was a huge increase in the numbers of vocations to the diocesan priesthood and to orders of religious sisters and brothers, but not very many for religious orders devoted to first evangelisation in continents like Africa. This was largely due to the need to provide for the Irish diaspora created by the famine and the constant emigration which would continue for a century. The demand for such priests continued through the nineteenth and most of the twentieth century. The numbers of young men opting to join congregations devoted to first evangelisation was rather small. Commenting on this, Fr Leman remarked very early on when writing to Fr Schwindenhammer: 'The Irish readily expatriate, but religious life has very little attraction for them ...' From his contacts with people like Dr Bartholomew Woodlock, Rector of All Hallows, and his predecessor Dr David Moriarty, now Bishop of Kerry, Fr Leman was to gain further insights into the Irish situation and the Irish mentality. To put it briefly he soon came to know that Irish students for the secular priesthood valued their freedom, their standard of living and their status. In this they had the backing of their parents who made sacrifices for them and expected to benefit from their advancement.[3] There was little to be gained by way of material benefit from devoting one's life to evangelisation in Africa.

At the time of the arrival of the Spiritans in Ireland, Maynooth College had 500 students, while All Hallows had 200. In the course of the next forty-one years and in spite of having three large secondary level colleges and two junior scholasticates, the Spiritans only managed to promote a total of 96 candidates to ordination. Although the original objective of Jules Leman and his confrères in coming to Ireland remained largely unfulfilled, the Irish Spiritan foundation had done much to change attitudes to the non-Christian missionary cause.[4]

In spite of heavy involvement in education, Fr Leman aided by Fr Jean Martin Ebenrecht made a lasting contribution to the promotion of foreign missions. Although he personally never had the opportunity of working on the foreign missions, Leman remained a missionary at heart until his death. From the very beginning he sought to interest the Irish people in the work of evangelisation of the people of Africa – a cause for which there was little enthusiasm in Ireland.

3. Leman to Schwindenhammer, 14 December 1859; Leman ms p 113, quoted in Farragher, *op cit*, pp 101-102
4. Edmund Hogan, *The Irish Missionary Movement*, pp 77-78

CHAPTER TWO

The search for autonomy

The Spiritans in Ireland were quite slow in setting up houses for
the senior cycle of formation which would entitle them to the
status of a Province. For studies in philosophy, theology and for
their novitiate year, Irish candidates were sent to France. The
fact that young Irishmen had to spend many years in training in
French seminaries and had to give sometimes up to five years as
prefects in Spiritan second level colleges, may not have been a
very attractive proposition for some candidates. As well as that,
the French Spiritans looked upon the Congregation as a French
institution and it was perceived as such in Ireland. The French
also feared that left to themselves Irishmen would opt more and
more for work among the Irish of the diaspora and that Africa
would not be high on their list of priorities. At times the Irish
were made to feel that they were second class citizens rather than
members of the same congregation. With no preparation for living in an international community it is not surprising that there
were occasional culture clashes, especially when Irish students,
and particularly the Brothers, were subjected to insensitive treatment when they failed to comply with the French norms of life.

Beginning around 1890 there were repeated requests to the
Mother House for houses of formation in Ireland and the setting
up of a fully fledged province. Many letters of the period (1890-
1900) mention the need for some 'works of formation' at senior
cycle.[1]

The General Chapter of 1896 marks a turning point for the
Congregation and for the Irish Province. It decreed that those
countries which supplied their own personnel were to become
Provinces. A Province would be composed of the necessary
houses of training for the clerical and lay aspirants, and a certain
number of communities and works.[2]

A start with the houses of formation was made in Portugal

---

1. IPA 'Irish Province Growing Pains', Introduction to Council meet-
ingwith Fr Grizard, 31 Jan-1 Feb 1897
2. Henry Koren, *Spiritans*, p 237

where a novitiate was opened in 1896. Under the direction of the highly capable Fr John O'Gorman, a novitiate was launched in the USA the following year. Ireland would have to await the outcome of a major visitation from the Mother House to examine its organisation and precarious financial state. However, there was an immediate change in administration.

Hitherto the Superior of Blackrock College was also the Principal Superior. Since 1889 these two posts had been held by Fr Jules Botrel, an exceptionally talented man with long experience and a placid disposition. When Fr Botrel was appointed Provincial Superior in August 1896, he handed over the function of Superior of Blackrock to Fr Larry Healy, the first Irishman to hold the post. It was a small change, but it signalled that the Congregation in Ireland had, after 37 years, reached a certain stage of development and required some fulltime administration. Fr Botrel addressed himself to the problem immediately. All was not well within the Irish Province even though the former Superior General, Mgr Ambrose Emonet, declared that his visit of all the Irish houses in 1893 had left him 'very satisfied and very consoled'.

Bishop Alexander Le Roy, who was elected Superior General by the chapter of 1896, sent Fr John Grizard, Master of Novices, as visitor to Ireland. He spent almost 20 days trying to sort out the problems of the Irish circumscription in early 1897. During the long meeting, Fr Grizard had met with Fr Botrel and the four members of his council; it emerged that two Irishmen were for locating the senior scholasticate in Rockwell. The two Frenchmen, Fr Botrel and Fr Ebenrecht, along with Fr Healy, would like to see houses, especially the Brothers' novitiate, located away from any of the colleges.[3]

The response of the Mother House was to direct the setting up of a senior scholasticate at the Lake House in Rockwell, with the Brothers' novitiate on the Spiritan property at Ryebrook near Lucan. This response was dictated by the necessity to cease further expenditure and use one of the existing houses, rather than purchase a separate property. Given the state of the build-

---

3. IPA, Minutes of Provincial Council meeting in Blackrock, 31 Jan-1 Feb 1897

ing in Rockwell and the difficulty in providing personnel, candidates from Ireland were to continue their studies in Chevilly until the senior scholasticate could be established in Rockwell.

At the same time a new community was to be set up to cater exclusively for the promotion of mission awareness with Fr Ebenrecht in charge. This was the beginning of the Mission Band, housed temporarily at Kimberley House, Booterstown Avenue.[4]

Mgr Le Roy was finally able to visit Ireland in July 1897 and he announced major changes. The communities were told to tighten up on religious observance, and to cut down on expenses to eliminate their heavy burden of debt. In anticipation of adverse political events in France, he provided for the opening of a senior scholasticate in Ireland at St Joseph's in Rockwell.

Many problems had to be solved before the Senior Scholasticate could be opened. The junior scholastics had to be accommodated at the Blackrock juniorate and at the boarding school in Rockwell. There was also the question of staffing. It was taken for granted that Fr Louis de Maison, Director of the juniorate in Rockwell, would become Director of the senior scholasticate. He made a number of very significant proposals, particularly that the new community be given independent status from the Superior of the college. However, some of his demands were deemed unreasonable and he thereby excluded himself. The Director finally appointed was Fr Paul Meistermann, who had been Director of the juniorate in Cellule in France. His assistant was Fr John Desnier, another Frenchman who had been on the staff in Blackrock. Both were dedicated men, but neither of them was prepared in any way for conducting a senior seminary or teaching the wide range of subjects in theology.

When Fr Meistermann arrived in Ireland in October 1898 he had to spend five weeks putting order on chaos. Even with a year and a half's notice no one had taken responsibility to get things in order. There seems to have been uncertainty as to who was to report for fulltime study at the new seminary. A further complication was caused by the fact that the cycle in theology being followed that year had already been done by those who had completed a year's theology in Chevilly. One of the greatest

4. IPA, Mother House to Fr Botrel, 17 Feb 1897

problems was that former Rockwell prefects were called on to
help out at the college while attending lectures in theology.
Among those who were called upon, much to the annoyance of
Fr Meistermann, were Joseph Shanahan, Johnny Byrne and Phil
O'Shea. In his end of year report Fr Meistermann made many
criticisms of the situation in Rockwell.

It was hoped that there would be an improvement in the new
academic year especially after the six weeks' visitation of Fr
Joseph Eigenmann.[5] At the end of his visitation he read a hard-
hitting letter to the assembled communities from Mgr Le Roy,
who was still worried about the alarming leakage of members of
the Congregation even among those ordained, and the difficulty
of getting Irish personnel for the missions of Sierra Leone,
Nigeria and East Africa. He also addressed the problems of the
senior scholasticate, which according to Meistermann's report
militated against serious study of – or respect for – theology. His
admonitions fell on deaf ears. There was no improvement.

A hard hitting in-depth report from Fr Meistermann in June
1900 convinced most people that the venture should be called
off. There is a very sobering remark in Meistermann's final report: 'They (the Irish Spiritans) were asking for a separate
Scholasticate for years and now they say it was undertaken with
undue haste. They have done too much talking; now they should
begin to listen and to act and be ready to make sacrifices if the
province is to thrive.'[6]

Mgr Le Roy agreed in mid-August 1900 that his presence in
Ireland was urgently required. He came, he listened, and then
made several important decisions. Fr Larry Healy who had retired the previous year as Superior of Blackrock was appointed
Provincial replacing Fr Botrel, a man of peace, who was felt not
to be capable of giving the leadership required. Fr Botrel was
appointed superior of Clareville, adjoining Blackrock and the
Provincial of the Province was now to reside at Clareville, not at
the college. This was a clear signal that the college was not the
centre. Clareville was also the new mission house and the centre
for the Mission Band.[7]

5. Bulletin General (BG), 20, p 144
6. Meistermann's final report quoted in: Farragher, *Shanahan*, p 107
7. BG, 118, Nov 1896

The Slow Road to Kimmage

The failure of the Rockwell experiment did not dampen the desire and the quest of Fr Healy and his Council to establish a novitiate and Senior Scholasticate in Ireland. On this matter they were unanimous. The major question continued to be the one of finance as the Irish communities carried a heavy burden of debt. At the July meeting of the Council in 1902 there was a long discussion on the setting up of a novitiate and senior scholasticate ranging over courses of study to the timing of the novitiate year and the advantages of the university courses. Since finances were a major problem only a house of philosophy and novitiate should be considered. When it came to finances they decided to ask the Mother House to allow a remission of the *Contribution Personelle,* and allow grants from the missions that had been supplied with personnel from Ireland such as Trinidad and Sierra Leone.

When it came to location they had two houses in mind. Glencairn, about four miles from Blackrock, had been visited. Drishane Castle, near Millstreet in Co. Cork, which had suitable buildings for a novitiate for clerics and Brothers, was favoured by the Council, if the Mother House would consent. It could be purchased for between five and six thousand pounds.[8]

Nothing came of this new drive for houses of formation, but the discussion on the desirability of having them continued for the next nine years. Mgr Le Roy made it clear that no direct help could be given by any of the missions for the project, but he was sure that the Mother House would allow £20 per year for each scholastic and novice. Although the houses in Ireland were in debt, the General Council favoured going ahead with the project which they estimated in 1904 would cost around £5,000.[9]

Events in France hastened the need for a new house. Government policy in France to suppress religious orders and congregations created a crisis for Spiritans during the years 1902-1904. Congregations and orders which could show that

---

8. Minutes of the Provincial Council Meeting, 8 July 1902 – hereafter referred to as Pro Co
9. Pro Co, 6 April 1904

they had been approved by successive French governments were exempt. The original Society of the Holy Spirit had been approved in 1726 and again in 1816. This approval had never been revoked. The French Prime Minister, however, had been advised that the Holy Spirit Congregation had ceased to exist in 1848 when it was merged with the Congregation of the Holy Heart of Mary, and so it was decreed by the French Council of State in February 1901 that the civilly recognised Congregation of the Holy Spirit had ceased to exist. This judgement was based on what the members of the Congregation themselves had publicly affirmed, namely, that Francis Libermann was their founder and First Superior General.[10]

The Congregation with many others was suppressed in March 1903. Mgr Le Roy, acting on the advice of the archivist, Fr Desiré Barillec, challenged the decision. A detailed study of the historical documents discovered that not only did the Congregation of the Holy Spirit date back to 1703 but that it still legally existed both civilly and canonically. As part of the merger with the Congregation of the Holy Spirit in 1848, Propaganda Fide had suppressed the Society of the Holy Heart of Mary whose members were told to join the Congregation of the Holy Spirit.[11] Eventually the Council of State reversed its decision which resulted in the legal recognition the congregation enjoys to this day.

In spite of this recognition it was still feared that at least twelve houses would be closed. The big question was: what would happen to Chevilly? If Chevilly were suppressed where would scholastics be housed? Should that happen, it was decided that another property must be acquired.[12]

In 1904 Mgr Le Roy visited Ireland and met with the Provincial Council on 23 June. Here he stressed the necessity of a house of refuge in case things got worse in France. Prior Park, Bath, England had already been proposed and Le Roy thought it was suitable. The house and grounds could be had for three years

10. Michael Kilkenny, 'A merger, An Attempted Takeover ... Turning points in the Spiritan Story', in *Spiritan Horizons*, Issue 5, Fall 2010, 21-33
11. Kilkenny, *op cit*, p 21
12. Wilfrid Gandhy, *History of the English Spiritan Province*, pp 27-29

at a rent of £220. A decision had already been taken to cease sending novices to France because of the adverse political situation. Prior Park could be used for the time being as a novitiate for clerics and brothers of the Irish Province. At this meeting Le Roy also drew attention to the necessity of a more active publicity to draw more members into the society.[13]

The novitiate at Prior Park was canonically created on 4 August 1904. The community was fully operative by mid-October. Mgr Le Roy, who had been looking for a director appointed the very energetic and capable President of Blackrock, Fr John Baptist Tuohill (John T.) Murphy from Castleisland, Co Kerry. Being a man of broad vision and endowed with a great missionary spirit, John T. Murphy envisaged an international English-speaking novitiate and scholasticate with Irish, English, Americans and French all being trained together for the English colonies.[14] Fr Thomas O'Brien from St Mary's College was appointed novice master for clerics with Fr Husser as assistant. Fr Joseph Lictenberger, a Frenchman from Alsace, became novice master for the brothers. He was later replaced by Dr Martin Croagh from Co. Tipperary.

Although houses of formation catering for English speakers had been set up in Prior Park, Fr Healy and the Provincial Council in Ireland had not abandoned the idea of a novitiate and scholasticate in Ireland. The General Chapter at Chevilly in June 1906 considered the matter and agreed in principle that Ireland should have its own novitiate and scholasticate. At this stage there were twelve candidates ready to begin their novitiate year.[15] Archbishop William Walsh of Dublin was approached by Frs Healy and Botrel to seek permission to buy a new property for the proposed novitiate and senior scholasticate of the Irish Province. The archbishop was not enthusiastic as he considered that the number of new foundations in the diocese had reached limits beyond which it was not prudent to go. He, therefore, advised Fr Healy to use one of the existing Spiritan properties for the project. As well as that he pointed out that there were already too many institutes in the Booterstown

13. Pro Co, 23 June 1904
14. Pro Co, 4 August 1904
15. Pro Co, 31 October 1906

and Blackrock area.[16]

While conceding the Archbishop's point, Fr Healy informed him that they had now thought of buying 'The Hermitage' in Rathfarnham which would be away from Blackrock.[17] Healy believed that the archbishop would indeed grant permission only to be informed by the Archbishop that he and his Council had come to the unfavourable conclusion that it would be difficult to grant permission to the Spiritans to open houses of formation while refusing others.[18] There the matter rested for the time being.

Discussion about providing a novitiate in Ireland continued during Fr Edward Crehan's term as Provincial, 1907-1910. In January Mgr Le Roy conveyed his views on the matter to Fr Crehan through Fr Anthony Zielenbach, the General Councillor. Fr Crehan was reminded firmly that the Archbishop of Dublin was not opposed to the erection of a novitiate on one of the existing Spiritan communities, but that he was opposed to the acquisition of a new house. The difficulty, he pointed out, lay with the Irish Spiritans who would not accept having a novitiate attached to Blackrock College.

Meanwhile, the novices and scholastics continued at Prior Park until this location was abandoned in 1907 due to an enormous increase in the rent. In 1906, Fr John T. Murphy had been appointed USA Provincial at the request of the confrères there. The Irish clerical novices returned to France in 1908 while the novitiate for brothers was transferred to the acquired property at Castlehead nearby, where Irish aspirants to the brotherhood continued until 1911.[19] Fr John Neville, was appointed to the General Council, the first Irishman to hold the post.

The Irish Spiritans remained adamant in their demand for houses of formation, especially a novitiate, but they still, one thinks quite rightly, refused to have them as annexes to a college. On 28 June 1910 Mgr Le Roy requested the Provincial, Fr Crehan, along with Fr Hugh O'Toole and Fr Thomas Pembroke to travel to Paris to discuss the problems of the Irish Province.

16. IPA, Archbishop Walsh to Fr Healy, 19 Oct 1906
17. Healy to Archbishop Walsh, 22 Oct 1906
18. IPA, Archbishop Walsh to Healy, 10 Nov 1906
19. Gandhy, *op cit*, pp 33-44, *passim*

Then in August 1910, in what was to prove an extremely significant move, the Mother House recalled Fr John T. Murphy from the USA to provide leadership for the Irish Province.

Fr Murphy may rightly be looked upon as the second founder of the Irish Province. With his usual great energy, he threw himself into this new task. Not only was he energetic, but he also had, as already noted, a very strong sense of mission. He urged the setting up of a more independent Provincial administration with more powers and responsibilities for members of the Province. Direct dependence on the Mother House left the Province without a credible centre of its own to plan its own affairs. Ireland still lacked the necessary houses of formation required for recognition as a Province, so Fr Murphy's first move was to provide a novitiate and senior scholasticate.

The year 1911 was to be one of intense activity. It began with a five-day extraordinary meeting of the Provincial Council along with fourteen other participants in Clareville from 3 to 7 January inclusive. In a wide-ranging report John T. Murphy outlined the merits and demerits of each of the colleges and other properties of the congregation and considered their suitability as centres for houses of formation. Two of the colleges, St Mary's and Rockwell, carried large burdens of debt. St Mary's had the added disadvantage of being 'too much in the city, too exposed to the public gaze, too limited in space … Moreover its debt and annual charges would fall on the Province once the day school is closed'. The advantages were, except for the chapel, fairly sufficient buildings. From the point of view of proximity to the new university the site was considered admirable. Rockwell was ruled out especially because of its remoteness, the unsuitability of its buildings and its large debt. If the sites at Clareville and Merrion were to be used it would entail extensive building.[20]

Despite the serious disadvantages with the property and its location much of the discussion which followed centred on the possibility of making one wing of St Mary's College available and suitable as a senior scholasticate for students of philosophy. But this would only be a temporary measure. Its proximity to

20. IPA, Fr Murphy's report: 'Schemes of the organisation of the Irish Province CSSp', January 1911

the university in Earlsfort Terrace gave it decided advantages as
it had been decided that all senior scholastics were to read for
the BA after completing the novitiate. The university course
generally was to be philosophy, but brighter students might
take other course such as classics, mathematics or science.[21]

In spite of all the discussion on using St Mary's there was a
very strong desire to locate the senior scholasticate entirely
away from the colleges, since the main object of any of the new
houses of formation was to foster the missionary rather than the
college spirit.[22] So when the Council met at the end of January
the decision to use St Mary's was reversed and Fr Murphy announced that he was in fact seeking permission from the
Archbishop of Dublin for a separate property for the novitiate
and scholasticate.[23]

Archbishop Walsh was again approached to request permission for the new proposed novitiate and house of studies. The
Archbishop gave approval for the purchase of Dunfillan House
in Rathgar but the Mother House refused. Fr Murphy was not to
be deterred so he set off for Paris on Friday 24 February with a
report from the Provincial Council as to why they should buy
Dunfillan House. Convinced by Fr Murphy's arguments, the
Mother House agreed to its purchase. But when Fr Murphy got
back to Ireland a week later Dunfillan had already been sold.

Fortunately, other properties came on the market, but the
final choice was Kimmage Manor, which had a magnificent and
suitable house and out-offices. It also had 69 acres of land at a
yearly rent of £147 and rates at £80. It was also near enough to
the city and only a mile from the tram terminus at Terenure. All
agreed it was an ideal location. Furthermore Fr Pembroke,
Superior of Rockwell, wrote that 'that amount of land near
Dublin is a regular gold mine'.[24] Even a cursory reading of the
Council minutes shows that the members had indeed given serious vetting to the property.

21. Pro Co, 3-7 January 1911
22. *Ibid*
23. Pro Co, 27 Jan 1911
24. Pembroke to John T. Murphy 25 March 1911; Pro Co, 7 April 1911

Even before the deal was completed, Fr Jules Botrel visited Kimmage with the intention of designing a chapel. Fr Ebenrecht gave a glowing account of the building after his visit to it with Fr Murphy: 'The house is a magnificent chateau' in the best state of preservation; a large farm, fields, out-offices, garden surround the mansion. Fr Ebenrecht is drawing up plans for a chapel to adjoin the dwelling house. The situation is an ideal one.' However, the chapel did not materialise for a long time.[25]

The Mother House approved of the transaction and moves were quickly made to provide personnel and finance. With the consent of the Archbishop of Dublin, Mgr Le Roy requested Rome to erect a novitiate for clerics and brothers. Permission was granted on 7 June 1911 and Brother Gerald Heffernan took possession of the property on 21 July 1911.[26]

---

25. *Blackrock Journal*
26. Pro Co, 7 June 1911

CHAPTER THREE

Novitiate and House of Philosophy 1911-1917

Kimmage opened as a novitiate and House of Philosophy on 2 September 1911. There were 14 clerical novices, 1 novice brother, 10 postulant brothers and, eventually, 11 senior scholastics. The superior of the new community was Fr John Stafford who had been director of the Juniorate in Blackrock from 1909-1911. Fr Michael A. Kelly was appointed Master of Novices. After his novitiate in France, Fr Kelly studied at the Academy of St Thomas in Rome where he was conferred with a Doctorate in Philosophy, and then proceeded to study for his licentiate in Theology at the Gregorian University. He had been a very successful director and teacher at the Juniorate in Castlehead. The Director of Philosophers was Fr Daniel D. Walsh from Skibbereen in Co. Cork who was ordained the previous year. Brother Malachy Fleming, who had completed his novitiate at Castlehead in 1909, was transferred to Kimmage with the novice brother and the postulant brothers.

Much of the work of preparing Kimmage for the new community was done by the priests and brothers. Brothers were to play a very important role in the general running and maintenance of the house and farm. Along with Brothers Gerald Heffernan and Malachy Fleming in the initial stage were Brothers Killian Melligan, Declan Mansfield and Joseph Winters. A year later, Brother Dismas Zimmermann arrived from Germany at the request of Fr Stafford who was looking for a good cook for Kimmage. He got a good one in Dismas who for many years was to do wonders in the kitchen in Kimmage and later in Blackrock.

The first solemn High Mass in Kimmage was on Sunday 3 September with Fr Murphy as celebrant. During Mass, Fr Murphy gave an instruction on the aims and ends of the community. That evening, Fr Botrel came from Blackrock to give solemn Benediction of the Blessed Sacrament. The large parlour nearest the entrance was used as a chapel. Two days later the novitiate officially began[1] under the direction of Fr Michael A.

---

1. IPA, Letter from Fr John T. Murphy to Fr Nicholas Brennan, 6 September 1911

Kelly who had already made his mark as a distinguished student, successful director, teacher and sportsman. One of his first novices described him as 'a cultured sympathetic priest, a distinguished preacher with a deep spirituality combined with a fine sense of humour and a beautiful singing voice'. He was also a splendid psychologist and a sympathetic listener.[2]

Among the first group of novices were Charles Heerey, future Archbishop of Onitsha in Nigeria, James Leen, later Archbishop of Port Louis, Mauritius, and Francis Griffin, who became Superior General in 1950. The scholastics included Edward Leen, John English, Peter Walsh, Nicholas O'Loughlin, Patrick Heerey, James Mellett, Bernard Fennelly, Eugene O'Connell and Michael O'Connor.

The superior of the new community, Fr John Stafford, was well known to most of the novices and scholastics as he had been Director of the Juniorate in Blackrock. He was a strict and stern man who almost worked himself to death for the next six years as superior and bursar trying to keep the community going, with a minimum of financial resources at his disposal. He used to say that be began Kimmage with £5 in his pocket. In 1917 he became Provincial Bursar, a post he held until 1937.

A short time after the community was established, the Provincial Administration moved from Clareville to Kimmage, an indication of the interest that Fr Murphy had in the new house of formation. On 4 October, Mgr Le Roy visited the community accompanied by Fr Anthony Zielenback, a General Councillor. Mgr Le Roy spoke to the whole assembled community and expressed his delight that a novitiate and senior scholasticate were established in Ireland.

As the year went by the details of community were worked out. Schedules and regulations were ready to hand. They were exactly the same as those followed in all the houses of formation in France. Rising for all was at 5.00 a.m., followed by Morning Prayer and Meditation from 5.15 a.m. until 6.00 a.m. Novices and students all assembled for Mass at 6.30 a.m followed by thanksgiving, study and then breakfast usually at 8.00 a.m.

---

2. *Missionary Annals*, October 1961, pp 4-8, and *Missionary Annals*, December 1936, pp 276-7.

Every fifteen-minute period of the day was worked out – times for prayer in common and in private, times for spiritual reading, times for manual labour – all interspersed with periods of free time. On most days there were classes or conferences on spirituality, liturgy, ascetical theology, regular law (canon law regulating religious life) or Latin given by the novice master or another member of the staff. Once a week, there was a welcome break from routine, when novices got out for a whole afternoon for a walk, usually in the countryside, though they did from time to time walk into the city to see the sights. Dinner was usually at 1.00 p.m. though there was some flexibility in the time. Supper was at 7.00 p.m. followed by recreation. Night prayer was at 8.30 p.m. and lights were put out at 9.00 p.m.

All categories in the community shared the same facilities for the first four years. The large parlour, now a classroom, on the right-hand side just inside the present entrance to the Manor was used as a chapel for everyone. The last room on the same side was used as a dining room. The large rooms on the top floor were dormitories. In all, there were 21 rooms in the building, some very large such as reception rooms, or parlours or drawing rooms. Others were modest-sized bedrooms and a few were little more than box rooms. Two were in the basement of the old eigtheenth-century building along with the kitchen. Such was the demand for space that portions of the attic were used as bedrooms. All, except the attic, are in full use to the present day mainly as offices, classrooms and meeting rooms for the Kimmage Development Studies Centre.

The original water supply for the house came from a deep well which is just under the granite step at the main entrance to the manor building. This was piped around the old house to a pump to the rear that is on the east side of the original building. Some time before 1929 the water came from the public water supply and was piped in from Whitehall Road through the old orchard, and entered the building near the Evans Chapel (Venerable Libermann oratory). A booster pump was installed in 1938 to pump the water to the new scholasticate building. Another supply was brought in around 1947 by the farm entrance from Whitehall Road. The whole system was upgraded at that time with hydrants, valves and metres. The sewerage system was local with a cesspit near where Marian House is now built. For many years, however, there were drawers of water (along with hewers of wood) to the various rooms and bathrooms.

What about lighting and heating? For lighting, each member of the community had an oil lamp with a glass globe. There were larger hanging oil lamps in the larger rooms for the community. In the early days a philosopher had the function of 'lampist' and his job was to light each lamp especially on winter mornings. That situation might explain the early to bed and early to rise policy. Electricity was installed in 1929.

One of the striking features of the old buildings is the number of chimneys and the number of flues to each chimney – nearly all had six flues. This was because there was no central heating. Every room in the house had a fireplace all of which had to be supplied with fuel and lit during the winter months. While the philosophers remained in Kimmage, supplying fuel and lighting the fires was their lot.[3]

The whole novitiate might be described as a period of initiation into the Spiritan missionary way of life. Formation was concerned with providing the novices with a clear idea of their religious and missionary vocation. They were also shown the means of arriving at the qualities required for such a vocation following the ideas and ideals of the Venerable Francis Libermann. For novice masters such as Fr Kelly and his immediate successors the spirituality of Francis Libermann was paramount. They themselves had had a thorough grounding in Libermann's spirituality from the days of French novice master, Fr John Grizard. Novices were also introduced to the spiritual teachings of Fr Louis Lallemont and of Alphonsus Rodriguez. The former work had a considerable influence on Libermann. The latter work was a rather strange mixture of ascetical teaching, illustrated with a host of pious myths and legends which novices read walking around what was called the 'Rodriguez Walk'. Its pious legends provided much light relief for most novices, who had enough common sense not to take them seriously. Other standard works were St Francis de Sales' *Introduction*

---

3. Novices' and Scholastics' Journals, *passim*

to the Devout Life; Abbé Constant Fouard, *Christ the Son of God*, and *St Paul and his Missions*. Overall novices were introduced to and trained to be missionaries in the best traditions of the congregation. Sound spiritual formation and personal discipline was of enormous importance to men who would have to face the rigours of living in totally different cultures and climates to bring the message of Christ to the poor and abandoned. The novitiate was seen as a power house of spiritual forces to prepare young men to spread God's kingdom on earth.

The regime for the philosophers was similar in many respects to that of the novices for the core elements of the daily schedule such as rising, prayers, meals, study and the hours set aside for manual labour. Since there was a strong emphasis by Fr Murphy and his Council on the necessity for university degrees for all students, not merely for those engaged in education at home and on the missions, the philosophers were sent to the newly opened University College Dublin (UCD). The philosophy course at UCD in those days was designed almost exclusively as a preparation for the study of theology, although Arts subjects such as English, Irish, Latin, Greek and French were included. As a young man Fr Murphy received grounding in the classics from his granduncle, Fr James Tuohill, and retained a great love for them all his life. He now had some of the best students brought back from France to qualify for degrees in science as well as classics and philosophy and a variety of other degrees in the Arts Faculty.

In September 1912, Fr Denis Fahey returned from Rome with doctorates in philosophy and theology. He took over as Director of Philosophy from Fr Dan Walsh who became novice master instead of Fr Kelly who was sent to the USA as part of the fundraising team. Fr Fahey took such a keen interest in the philosophy course in UCD that he attended the course himself. He was not entirely satisfied and decided to supplement the course in Thomistic Philosophy given at Kimmage. On completion of their studies in philosophy the students were sent to Chevilly in France for theology.

CHAPTER FOUR

An accommodation crisis

Accommodation reached almost crisis point from the outset. With some forty-four people in the Manor House, conditions must have been really cramped. Even before the final purchase of Kimmage, a far-sighted Fr Murphy had plans drawn for an extension. In the final plan there were eighteen bedrooms, a small oratory, dining room, study hall, reception room and novice master's office. It was some time before the new building commenced. The work was undertaken by M. Glynn of 12 North Brunswick Street, who contracted to have it finished by the middle of August 1913. There were considerable delays, not least because of the building strike in the autumn of 1913. The building was not completed until the end of January 1915 and it was solemnly blessed on 2 February of that year. This extension was henceforth used for the novices, and is known still as the old novitiate. Even with the new extension accommodation would continue to be a huge issue for years to come.

The Drexel Agreement

Fr Murphy had big plans, but limited financial resources. Purchasing the property, maintaining the community and paying for the new extension were a huge drain on financial resources. Little help was received from the Mother House, the colleges paid their levy but this was altogether insufficient so Fr Murphy turned his thoughts to the USA where he had been Provincial for four years, 1906-1910.

During both his earlier years (1887-1893), in the USA, and while he was Provincial there, Fr Murphy had been in contact with Mother Katherine Drexel, the daughter of a powerful finance company owner in Philadelphia. She went on to become the foundress of the Sisters of the Blessed Sacrament for Indians and Coloured People. Along with being extremely rich she lived a very saintly life and was beatified on 28 November 1988 and canonised on 1 October 2000. While he was Provincial in the USA, Fr Murphy had co-operated with Mother Drexel in providing priests for black people in parishes in the US. Now in

1912 Fr Murphy planned on sending the members of the Mission Band to do fund-raising in the USA. He himself set out for New York in April of that year. Fr Eugene Phelan, who had succeeded him as US Provincial, approached Mother Katherine on behalf of Fr Murphy. He could report in May 1912: 'I succeeded in having her give $6,000 to the new building in Kimmage Manor on the condition that you give to the American Province each year a newly professed scholastic beginning with September 1912 ... Next year she will give an additional $4,000 for the same purpose on the condition that you send us each year two newly professed scholastics. Our Province binds itself to employ such members after their consecration in the coloured ministry.'

By the end of October 1912 the 'Drexel Agreement' was completed. According to the agreement the Irish Province would supply the American Province with one scholastic after profession each year for 20 years, to complete his studies in the American scholasticate and afterwards be engaged in works among the 'coloured' people of the US. In return Mother Drexel would contribute $6,000 annually for the erection of the Kimmage novitiate and scholasticate. Fr Murphy was not entirely happy with the agreement and the Irish Provincial Council was opposed to it, thinking it financially unsound and odious in other ways. The Mother House was slow in approving but finally it accepted the contract. The first $6,000 draft was dispatched on 5 November 1912.[1]

Meanwhile the Mission Band was also at work fund-raising under the direction of Fr Cornelius (Con) O'Shea, assisted by the very able preacher Fr Michael A. Kelly who had been novice master. At the end of their first year of operations they were able to forward £1,000 to Fr Murphy. Seven months after the completion of the novitiate, Mgr Le Roy expressed his pleasure that the novitiate/scholasticate had been built and paid for.[2]

Even with the new extension Kimmage was still overcrowded. The situation became acute with the outbreak of the First World War when students of theology were hindered from going to France for their studies. Kimmage had to accommodate

---

1. IPA, Leo Leyden, 'The Drexel Agreement', unpublished article
2. IPA, A. Le Roy to the members of the Irish Provincial Council

novices, philosophers, theologians, brothers and members of staff and the Provincial administration. In the midst of all this, Fr John T. Murphy who had done so much to launch the novitiate and scholasticate and re-orientate the whole province was appointed Bishop of Port Louis in Mauritius in 1916. His successor was Fr Con O'Shea, Director of the Mission Band since 1912.[3] One of his first acts was to close St Mary's College and turn it into a senior scholasticate for philosophers, providing much needed space for everyone. For over 15 years the General Council had spoken out about St Mary's which it considered a mistake. It had been a serious financial liability and absorbed a lot of personnel who were needed elsewhere. Moreover it had deviated from the purpose for which it was founded.

It is important to remark at this point that the General Council had been reminding the Irish Spiritans on a regular basis that they had allowed themselves to be drawn aside from the purpose of the congregation. There was an urgency about the need for the Irish Province to provide as many personnel as possible to English-speaking missions. At that point in history a great movement towards the missions to the non-evangelised was discernible in every Christian country. There was concern that it was the Protestants who were giving 'an example as glorious for them as it is humiliating for us'. Although the Congregation was by its nature and end apostolic, it was felt that Ireland was not playing its part.[4] This must have been a sad moment for Fr John T. Murphy who had contributed so much to Mission Animation.

Kimmage buildings had become totally inadequate and there was no question of building during war time. It was agreed that the farm and gardens would continue to contribute pro rata to the scholasticate in St Mary's. To ease the congestion in Kimmage, Fr O'Shea moved the Provincial administration to St Mary's. Early in July the Kimmage scholastics began preparations for the move to St Mary's and the exodus was completed

3. BG, 28, p 351, 18 July 1916
4. IPA, Provincial Ireland, 'Propositions relating to a new organisation, Paris, 16 June 1914; A Le Roy to members of the Irish Provincial Council, 13 August 1915; see also Pro Co, 16 June 1914

by 6 August.[5] Just at this time those scholastics who were still studying in France were recalled to Kimmage. At last the Irish Province had all its houses of formations, but the situation was far from satisfactory. The return of the theology students to Kimmage added a further strain on the accommodation since the course in theology lasted four years. There were constant complaints that facilities in general were inadequate.

Although the students of philosophy lived in St Mary's they maintained close contact with Kimmage and returned on a regular basis for manual labour, taking part in the usual farm work of planting, harvesting and thrashing. They also came for games.

For a time the Kimmage farm was managed as provincial property by the Provincial Bursar. This was done to ensure an impartial and equitable distribution of farm produce between the Kimmage and St Mary's communities.

The Brothers' Novitiate continued at Kimmage. It was recognised, however, that Kimmage was not an ideal place for the overall formation of the brothers since it lacked workshops and other facilities for training in a trade or profession. In 1920 Fr Edmund Cleary was appointed novice master for the brothers and bursar for the whole community, a post he held until 1933.

Meanwhile the Easter Rising had taken place beginning on Easter Monday, 24 April 1916. While the journals give daily accounts of the Rising, they show little of the reaction of staff, students or novices. Fr Murphy, who still resided at Kimmage as Provincial, was no champion of the Rising. He was in fact an ardent Home Ruler. He did, however, pay generous tribute to the leaders, many of whom, like Thomas MacDonagh and Éamon de Valera, he had known personally. The progress of the Rising was recorded daily by both novices and scholastics who were well aware of what was happening. From the very first day they heard the sound of gunfire from around the city and knew that the Irish Volunteers had seized the greater part of Dublin and floated the flag of the Irish Republic over their headquarters at the GPO. On Friday, 28 April, St Mary's was occupied by the military and the staff dispersed. Students at Kimmage

5. Scholasticate Journal, Vol III, 1915-1918

prepared six rooms for them, but only Fr Laurence Healy availed of the offer, while the rest went to Blackrock. The postal service was disrupted and there was practically no communication between the city and the suburbs. The bursar became anxious about provisions and all were put on a 'war allowance' in the dining room on the Tuesday of Easter week. Walks outside of the community were restricted. Late on Saturday a telephone message was received saying that peace had been made, though cannon and rifle fire continued. As it turned out the message was premature. There were indications, however, on Sunday evening that some arrangements had been reached.

The university was due to reopen on Tuesday 2 May after the Easter recess, but nobody was allowed to enter the city area without a special permit from the military authorities. Students ventured into the city on the afternoon of Monday 8 May to see especially that part of it which had been the scene of the encounter between the volunteers and the military. After a five-week break lectures at the university resumed on Wednesday 10 May.

The Rising failed to take on a national dimension which was very reassuring for the military commanders. Their reaction was swift. Many of the rebels were tried by court martial and ninety were sentenced to death. Despite the mounting volume of protest fifteen were executed including all the signatories to the Proclamation. Executions began on 3 May and ended a little over a week later. De Valera, alone of the military commanders had his sentence commuted, not as is sometimes claimed, because of his American birth, but because the politicians had finally regained the initiative from the military. One of the first to be executed on 3 May was Thomas Mc Donagh, former pupil and teacher at Rockwell and Professor of English at UCD. On Saturday 3 June 1916 there was a requiem Mass for Mc Donagh in the university church which was attended by the Kimmage university students, many, perhaps all, of whom would have known him.

The executions caused revulsion. Within a very short time there was a massive swing in public opinion regarding the Rising. All those executed were Catholics, and this, coupled with the undoubted piety of some of them, soon led to a cult growing up in their memory. This was not without its repercussions in Kimmage. Just one year after the Rising, on Easter Tuesday, 17 April 1917, though free to go where they wished, each group, even the Directors, was found somehow to converge at the graves of the Easter week 'Martyrs' in Glasnevin. The record however, includes the comment: 'Peace to their memory and a truce to their policy.' Some months later as the philosophy students were passing through Newtown Mount Kennedy on their way home from an outing they got news of the election in East Clare. The journalist wrote: 'Our friend Dev got in by a majority of 3,000'.[6]

The nationalist mood continued to grow in Kimmage and was highlighted in the community's response to the death of 17-year-old Kevin Barry, executed for killing two British soldiers collecting bread in North King Street, Dublin. 'Another tragic death united us all in prayer today', the students' diarist reported in the Missionary Annals. 'Many masses were offered in our communities this morning for the gallant Kevin Barry, who was, up to a few weeks ago, a pupil in one of our Colleges (St Mary's), and whose name is now inscribed on the list of those who died for Ireland. God send us more like Kevin Barry. He is a splendid type of Catholic Irishman. He is a worthy model in every sphere of life – in church, in army or in state: unselfish, brave and true'.[7]

During 1916-17 many changes took place in Kimmage. A new era began, with the appointment in August 1916 of Fr Hugh Murray Gunn Evans as novice master and superior. He was to retain both posts until 1933. He was already a man of wide experience. He had served in St Mary's Rathmines, as bursar in Rockwell College, Director of Juniorate at St Joseph's, a member of the Mission Band, bursar in Blackrock and superior in Rockwell. Fr Dan Walsh, who had been novice master, now became Director of Scholastics at Kimmage.[8]

When the philosophers moved to St Mary's in August 1917, Fr Walsh took over in Kimmage as Director of Theologians. In

6. *Scholastics Journal*, vol III. (This gives us some insight into the change of opinion among the students.)
7. MA extracts, November 1920, p 15
8. BG, 28, p 352

the autumn of 1917 Irish scholastics studying in Chevilly were recalled to Kimmage. At last Ireland had all the houses of formation which entitled it to become a province. Fr Herbert (Bertie) Farrell was appointed to teach moral theology in Kimmage in 1917. A man who was to be one of the longest serving members on the teaching staff, Fr Bernard Fennelly, was also appointed to Kimmage where he taught mostly Canon Law and Sacred Scripture. A bonus for Fr Fennelly would have been the promulgation of the new Code of Canon Law on 15 September 1917 to come into effect on Pentecost Sunday the following year.

As with the philosophers, novices now mixed fairly regularly with the theology students, especially for regular evenings of music recitals, usually organised by Fr Evans.

To a great extent moral theology dominated the overall theology programme. The courses followed were those to be found in the traditional manuals. The text that influenced generations of students was that of Hieronymus Noldin, SJ, *Theologia Moralis*, Vols I-III. First published in 1880, it ran to 26 editions. There were other manuals of moral theology such as those published by Augustine Lemkuhl, who also published a volume on cases of conscience especially useful for confessors. A favourite with most professors of moral theology was Arthur Vermeersch SJ, Professor of Moral Theology at Louvain University. He was admired even by modern theologians for his creativity and his rejection of moral minimalism. Besides, the framework of his moral theology was the virtues rather than the Ten Commandments. Theology students in Kimmage were regularly given cases of conscience to solve and if a good discussion got under way it could last for the duration of these classes.[9]

Dogmatic theology again was guided by the Latin manuals. Until at least the 1960s it was taught mainly in Latin. The most popular manual was that of the Belgian, Mgr Gerardus Cornelis Van Noort, published in 7 volumes or tracts, each tract dealing with a specific area of dogmatic theology. Studying dogma wasn't confined merely to lectures. From the beginning there appeared what was called 'The circle'. In later times students often wondered why it was called a 'circle'. Many will be sur-

9. *Scholastics Journal*, vol III

prised to find that it was group discussion. Students broke up into groups of six to discuss the mysteries of theology. This was sometimes referred to as a 'dogmatic chat'. In later years 'the circle' was a dreaded public questioning in Latin of a few students for the duration of a class. Sometimes students and professor had a 'Theological Conference' during which a student read a paper on a particular topic. This was followed by a free-for-all discussion.

When the faculty was established in 1917, Fr James Murphy was appointed to teach dogmatic theology. As a student he had studied theology at the Gregorian University where he was conferred with a Doctorate in Divinity. Henceforth he was known to many generations of students as 'The Doc' Murphy. During his long stint as Professor of Theology he was noted for his conservatism. A student under Cardinal Billot at a time when the stress was very much in combating the errors of modernism, Fr Murphy set great store by accepted orthodoxy and stamped out any deviations therefrom. Indeed his teaching method, which was directed very much at achieving success in the diocesan vicariate examinations, dampened any great interest in further reading or personal research then or later. Outside of the lecture hall 'the Doc' was a different man, kind, gracious and good humoured, perhaps a bit shy, a man who never sought power or the limelight in any way.[10]

Fr Bernard Fennelly, already mentioned, may indeed hold the record as the longest-serving staff member in Kimmage. He was among the last of the Irish Spiritans to be ordained in France, in 1916. He had been among the first group of philosophers in Kimmage in 1911. He taught mostly Canon Law and scripture.

Canon Law was regarded as an important subject, but sacred scripture was at that time the Cinderella of theological studies. Without ever having done any special course in Canon Law Fr Fennelly became a recognised authority in that discipline and was a *peritus* of Vatican II. Although the theology students would eventually move to Blackrock in 1924, he remained on in Kimmage as confessor to the novices and as chaplain to the Presentation Sisters in Terenure. He lived all his years in Kimmage until his death in October 1991. He was affectionately known as 'The

10. *Irish Spiritans Remembered* (ISR).

Bar', and was much sought after as a confessor and adviser by generations of scholastics, who found him a never-failing source of encouragement.[11]

Kimmage now had a full complement of staff for both novitiate and house of theology. As already noted, Fr Dan Walsh became Director of Theologians when the philosophers moved to St Mary's. In the midst of all this change Ireland along with the rest of the world was ravaged by the outbreak of the great influenza epidemic which struck between the spring of 1918 and early 1919.

An estimated 20,000 people died in Ireland as a result of the epidemic.[12] It made its first appearance in the Kimmage Community towards the end of October 1918. Then the community was thoroughly shocked when the director, Fr Walsh, was rushed to St Vincent's Hospital suffering from acute appendicitis. He had been operated on successfully, when he was suddenly affected by the symptoms of the dreaded flu, to which he succumbed on Tuesday, 19 November 1918. He had to be coffined immediately and was buried next day in Kill O' the Grange cemetery in the presence of the communities from Kimmage and Blackrock. Such was the state of the country and city at the time that only two horse-drawn cabs were available to carry people to the funeral. Requiem Mass took place the following day in Blackrock College attended by a good number of secular priests and members of religious communities. Only three members of Fr Walsh's family were able to attend, his father and his two brothers. Honouring his unselfish nature, a memorial to Fr Walsh was erected to the south of the Manor buildings bearing the inscription *nunquam sibi placuit.*[13]

Reporting the death to Mgr Le Roy, Fr O'Shea wrote: 'There is a great void left in the province. Though so young he was a man of great promise: gentle, balanced in temperament, gifted with solid judgement, highly intelligent and eminently practical. He carried out the duties of his delicate charge with the touch of the master and with such moderation'.[14]

11. ISR
12. Diarmuid Ferriter, *The Transformation of Ireland, 1900-2000*, p 185
13. *Scholastics Journal*
14. ISR pp 516-17

Immediately the Provincial Council appointed Fr John Kearney as Director of Theologians. All the students were familiar with him, and as the journalist wrote: 'We were happy under his saintly direction. The place of our departed Director has been worthily filled.' Fr Kearney taught Ascetical Theology and Regular Law to the novices. Fr Bertie Farrell now took over the classes in Moral Theology taught by Fr Walsh.

Studies and Mission Animation
The range of subjects taught in the house of theology was much the same as in any other seminary in Ireland or Europe. Programmes were fairly standard and candidates preparing for ordination had to satisfy the demands of the local ordinary as to competence in theology. Although Kimmage was a seminary for training priests for mission mostly in Africa the courses being taught there were similar in all respects to the courses being taught to those who were going to exercise pastoral ministry in Ireland. There was no course in missiology or in social and cultural anthropology. Whatever references there were to the church's mission *ad gentes* were to be found very briefly in the standard works on the theology of the church. Sociology, social and cultural anthropology were still in their infancy and had made little impact in Ireland. This gives rise to a number of questions: What vision did staff and students have of mission? What was the mission of the church? What was the role of the missionary among non-Christian peoples? How were staff and students oriented towards, and prepared for, work among peoples with entirely different customs, cultures, language and religion?

Those students who had gone to France and studied in the houses of the congregation there had the great advantage of meeting a constant stream of veteran missionaries from many parts of Africa, who related their experience to the students at all levels. These men were not mere storytellers with exotic tales about exotic people. They did, of course, tell of their successes and failures, but they also expounded on the problems of conveying the gospel message to people of different cultures and the necessity of learning the local languages. Many of them were frequent writers of articles for missionary magazines and none more than Mgr Alexander Le Roy who was Superior General from 1896-1926.

Le Roy was the first missionary to hold the post of Superior General. He was a man of vast experience, having worked first in houses of formation in France, then as a missionary and teacher in Pondicherry in India. Eventually he was appointed to the immense vicariate of Bagamoyo in modern Tanzania. There he travelled far and wide, making exploratory trips which, even with today's transport, are daunting ventures, to determine the best locations for new missions. He was a gifted writer, linguist, ethnologist, and cultural anthropologist. With his remarkable powers of observation and empathy with people he was able to record in precise detail the customs, culture and elements of the religion of the peoples he visited. He used his spare time to publish a series of interesting and widely-read books and articles about his work and studies and these soon made his name a byword with all who were interested in Africa. His famous work *La Religion des Primitifs* (1909) received an excellent review in the *American Anthropologist* by Frederick Starr, professor of Anthropology at Chicago University.[15] Le Roy also acquired vast knowledge and experience during his three years as Vicar Apostolic of the Two Guineas in West Africa.

As already noted, his appointment as Superior General marked a turning point in the Congregation. Not only did he encourage the setting up of new independent provinces, he also provided constant animation, exhortation and inspiration. He was passionate about the missionary end of the Congregation. Those who came in contact with him could not but be affected by his sincerity and enthusiasm.

This orientation towards mission, knowledge of mission history and missionary activity was conveyed to the novices and students of theology in a variety of ways. As part of their novitiate programme novices received instruction in the history of the congregation and its missions. Most of the emphasis in these early years would have been on the life and writings of Francis Libermann, with little mention of Claude Poullart des Places. It must be noted, however, that Henri Le Floch's *Claude Francois*

---

15. *American Anthropologist* NS, 13, 1911 pp 144-5

Poullart des Places, was read in French in the early days in Kimmage for novices and scholastics. Spiritans like Fr Hugh Evans and Fr Dan Walsh who had experienced Fr John Grizard directly or indirectly would have known that the driving force of the Congregation was the spiritual and apostolic teaching of Libermann, a matter which has been dealt with at length in a number of English publications in recent years (e.g. Christy Burke, *No Longer Slaves*; Tony Geoghegan, 'Apostolic Life', in *Spiritan Horizons,* Issue 3, Fall 2008). For Libermann the role of the Holy Spirit was central to any mission spirituality. He saw his own project as entirely the work of the Holy Spirit, and the way in which the Spirit operates cannot be predetermined. One must be constantly open to the inspiration of the Spirit. Listening to the Spirit speaking to us in the concrete situations of life became the dominant note in Libermann's mission spirituality.

Libermann's major concern was to promote the development of the African people by providing them with a message of hope. The guiding missionary principle was the establishment of an indigenous church and not just the baptism of as many as possible. 'The purpose of the mission is permanently to implant our holy religion by beginning the construction of the edifice of a canonically established church.' Therefore the church must have a definite mission policy with careful planning for the future. Fundamental to this plan was the formation of an indigenous ministry. From the outset the missionaries had to be convinced of the necessity of forming local clergy drawn from a Christian community. The mission had to begin with community and continue by building community. Therefore the first means to achieve this purpose was to be the missionary's personal holiness, preserved and supported by community life. 'The people of Africa will not be converted by the work of clever and capable missionaries, but through the holiness and sacrifice of their priests.'[16] Libermann's insistence on the establishment of an indigenous church stemmed from the knowledge that many flourishing missions established in the past had collapsed because these communities did not have the stable force of a church. These same ideas were expressed by Pope Pius XI in his

16. Burke, *op cit*, Chap 6, *passim*

encyclical on missions, *Rerum Ecclesiae*, while Benedict XV had stressed the training of local clergy in *Maximum Illud*.

A great motivating force running through the encyclicals and the missionary magazines was the plight of immense multitudes of people who dwelt in darkness and the shadow of death. The number of non-believers was estimated in 1919 to be one billion. 'The pitiable lot of this stupendous number of souls,' was for Benedict XV a source of great sorrow and he yearned to share with these unfortunates the divine blessings of the Redemption.[17] Popular preaching often put the case more graphically and simplistically, by portraying the work of the missionary as rescuing these abandoned souls from eternal damnation.

As well as magazines, encyclicals and other books on mission which were read to the novices and students of theology there were also the frequent visits of missionaries home on leave. The journals for both communities make frequent reference to these visits and to the talks and discussions which took place providing them with most of their insights into the work in Africa. A regular visitor during his sojourns in Ireland was Mgr Joseph Shanahan, Prefect Apostolic of Southern Nigeria from 1905, and who was made Vicar Apostolic in 1920. Mgr Shanahan was a gifted speaker and could hold an audience spell-bound for hours. Novices and students sometimes forgot to ring the community bell to move on to the next community exercise when he was speaking.

Another entertaining speaker was Fr Thady O'Connor who enlivened his talks with plenty of anecdotes and slides shown with a magic lantern, but he also got down to serious talk on very practical matters such as training catechists and the setting up of and the managing of teacher-training colleges. When Fr O'Connor was no longer able to continue his missionary work in Nigeria because of ill health, Bishop Shanahan unreservedly recommended him for the task of mission animation throughout the country. There were many others like Fr Henry Gogarty, later Vicar Apostolic of Kilimanjaro, Fr Pat Whitney, one of the diocesan priests who volunteered for Southern Nigeria, in re-

---

17. *Maximum Illud*, 5-7

sponse to the appeal by Mgr Shanahan, and who later went on to found the Missionary Society of St Patrick (Kiltegan Fathers).

The *Missionary Annals*, already referred to, was launched in August 1919 as *The Missionary Record of the Holy Ghost Fathers*. This title had to be changed after a few months when it was discovered that the Oblates had already had a magazine entitled *The Missionary Record*. The main purposes of the *Missionary Annals* was mission animation and fund-raising. It took its inspiration from *The Far East*, the missionary magazine of the newly founded Missionary Society of St Columban. The very first edition of the *Missionary Annals* in August 1919 carried an editorial which emphasised the fact that all missionary activity and missionary glories were not in the past. 'There is a not less glorious present being achieved in pagan Africa and elsewhere by Irish religious priests compelled by love of the Divine Redeemer to bring good tidings to many who were sitting in darkness and in the shadow of death' (Luke 1:79). Subtle parallels were made between the idealism and heroism of those involved in the current struggles for freedom and the greater battle with the forces of Satan by those who set out to conquer souls and free them from the clutches of evil. Missionaries were seen as doing battle with Satan, clad in the armour of their poverty and armed only with the Cross. 'These are the true heroes of our race.' There was a reference to 'A glorious death on the field of battle, and a grave in that soil which has witnessed to his apostolic labours'.[18] As time went on reference to the inspiration to be drawn from the idealism and heroism of those involved in the struggle for freedom became more explicit as can be seen from the obituary of Kevin Barry referred to earlier.

The articles in the magazine were of a high quality and that standard was maintained throughout its history and later when it became known as *Outlook*. The magazine provided an invaluable service in the areas of mission animation and it is still possible to meet Spiritans whose inspiration to become missionaries came from the *Missionary Annals*. In time it could prove to be a valuable source of income to finance the growing number of students who were opting for the religious missionary way of

18. *Missionary Record*, August 1919, editorial; see also E. Hogan, *Irish Missionary Movement*, p 147

life.

The publication of the first issue of the *Missionary Record* co-incided with the Missionary Exhibition at the Donnybrook Fair. The inspiration for the venture came from Sr Joseph Conception Vavasour, Superior of the Sisters of Charity at Merrion Home for the Blind. Its purpose was to raise funds for the missions headed by Bishops O'Gorman and Neville, and Fr Shanahan. This exhibition must have been the first public demonstration of support for the foreign missions at parish level. The senior scholastics from Kimmage, then on holidays at Blackrock along with those from St Mary's, manned the Missionary Exhibition. Ten thousand copies of the *Missionary Record*, which carried a front page advertisement for the event, were disposed of during the fair.[19]

Every issue of the *Missionary Annals* was read in the novices' and students' dining rooms. Each month there was a short article by one of the theology students under the title 'A Student's Diary' and later 'Kimmage Diary'. The houses of formation were given prominence in every issue, especially issues which dealt with ordinations and the progress of buildings in Kimmage.

The ordination of Joseph Shanahan as Bishop in Maynooth College on 6 June was another great boost to foreign missions for the whole country and for the congregation and for Kimmage novices and students. Shanahan was conscious that Ireland had given Nigeria its first Vicar Apostolic and in fact from then onward people began to associate Shanahan with the traditional image of St Patrick, Ireland's national Apostle. An element of surprise at the ordination was the singing for the first time of the *Missionary Hymn*, composed for the occasion by Fr Jim Burke, then a teacher at Blackrock, at the suggestion and with help from Fr John Kearney, Director of the Theologate in Kimmage. The music for it was based on a melody from Charles Gounod's 'Redemption'.[20] In both music and words the Holy Ghost *Missionary Hymn* has inspired generations of students with love and zeal for the foreign missions. The appointment of Fr Edward Leen at this time to Southern Nigeria, at the suggestion of Bishop Shanahan, was seen as a triumph for the missionary spirit, especially by

19. *Missionary Record*, July-August 1919; Farragher, *Shanahan*, pp 154-5
20. Farragher, *Shanahan*, 172-3

Shanahan.

On 21 January 1921 the Spiritan Communities in Ireland were formally declared to be a Province, sixty two years after the arrival of the first Spiritans in Ireland. Later that year ill-health brought about the resignation of Fr Con O'Shea as Provincial. At the height of the Civil War he died in Cork on 28 September 1922. He was succeeded by Fr Joseph Byrne, a very gifted man with doctorates in philosophy and theology from Rome, who served as a missionary in Sierra Leone for 5 years. In 1910 he was transferred to the USA to serve as novice master in Ferndale, and later become director and superior of the seminary there. Fr Byrne had very clear ideas about the purpose of the congregation – it was exclusively missionary.

Almost immediately after taking up office, Fr Byrne began a thorough examination of all the works of the Province, whose financial state appalled him. There was to be tightening up all round. Formation of missionaries became a major preoccupation with him. It was clear that something would have to be done to provide extra accommodation for novices and scholastics.

At the time, a lot of criticism was being voiced about the philosophy course at UCD, and it was felt that a better course could be done in two years in a house of the Spiritans' own. No other order had students at UCD except the Oblates. Dissatisfaction with the course was also expressed by the Professors at Clonliffe and All Hallows, the two major seminaries in Dublin. Apart from the perceived inadequacies of the course there were other reasons, not least financial, for not continuing at UCD. The total sum for fees came to over £300 per year and the Province could not afford this. The outcome was that students of philosophy residing in St Mary's Rathmines and later in Blackrock were no longer sent to the university for degrees of any kind. Students now read their philosophy courses at home and the course was reduced from three years to two.

There was great dissatisfaction with this decision among some members of the Council and throughout the Province. Their argument was that missionaries should be educated men with at least a BA degree that would qualify them for secondary school teaching. There was also the advantage of the extra 'polish' they could get by attending university and meeting professors and others of national reputation.[21]

The next major issue to be addressed was that of buildings. Serious thought was given to erecting a scholasticate in Kimmage for students of philosophy and theology with a separate building for novices. With increasing numbers of novices and scholastics, another accommodation crisis was looming for 1923-24. The solution was to move the theology students from Kimmage to the Castle in Blackrock for the new academic year in 1924. This was to be a temporary measure, for just a year.

In February/March 1924 Fr Byrne set up a committee to draw up 'A Review of the History and Development of the Irish Province of the Congregation of the Holy Ghost and the Immaculate Heart of Mary 1859-1924'. The members of the committee were Fr Laurence Healy, Fr John Kingston, Fr James Keawell, Fr Patrick Heerey and Fr James Leen.[22] The final document, which shows the influence of Fr Byrne himself, is totally and unambiguously pro mission in its thrust. 'We are exclusively a missionary Congregation. Everything in our life must be done for the missions, at least indirectly.' The big problem facing the Province at that time was how to find personnel to supply the various vicariates they were committed to evangelising: Sierra Leone, Southern Nigeria, Zanzibar, Kilimanjaro and Bagamoyo. Having critically examined all the works of the province, the document recommended the closing of the college in Rockwell. Fr Byrne stressed that Rockwell College was not being suppressed but transformed into a house of formation. He envisaged that it would become a large Missionary College housing all our junior and senior scholastics and the Brothers' novitiate. This could be an immediate solution to the accommodation crises facing the Province, which could also be saved the expense of putting up a senior scholasticate, a brothers' novitiate and a community chapel in Kimmage. Fr Byrne gave carefully thought-out arguments for and against this proposal, but his arguments for the venture were much stronger than those against. The formation and academic staff were totally opposed to such a move away from Dublin. They believed it would be a

---

21. Pro Co, 3 July 1923.
22. Pro Co, 24 March 1924

retrograde step and certainly very damaging to the intellectual and cultural formation of future missionaries.[23]

The idea was dropped and the Blackrock solution was adopted, but only as a temporary measure. The Castle at Blackrock College would be given over to the senior scholastics for one year, while the whole question of building at Kimmage would be given serious thought.

The move to Blackrock came just in time. On Friday, 22 August 1924 nineteen new novices, the biggest number ever, arrived in Kimmage. They took over the quarters usually occupied by the theologians. During the following week the property of the theologians, mainly furniture and books, was moved to Blackrock by horse and cart.[24] In the meantime, Fr Evans in Kimmage had already begun to get plans for further extensions.

Fr Byrne and the Provincial Council continued to address the issue of accommodation. In the autumn of 1924 just as scholastics were settling into the Castle in Blackrock, Willow Park property came on the market. It was offered to the Spiritans for £6,300. Alternatively they could have the house, grounds and gardens for an annual rent of £200 and an entry fine of £2,000. Some proposed that the property should be taken without the house, while others suggested that the house could be used for returned missionaries. Fr Byrne was opposed to the purchase on financial grounds. As he set off to Paris to advise the Generalate on this matter he delayed for some days in England. Meanwhile a telegram arrived in Paris with the message: 'Willow Park auction tomorrow; purchase 'yes' or 'no'.' Fr Edward Crehan, then attached to the General Council advised sending an affirmative response by telegram. The deed had been done by the time Fr Byrne arrived in Paris.[25] Willow Park was eventually used to house the students of philosophy who moved there from St Mary's in February 1925.

23. Pro Co, 3 April 1924, Memorandum of Academic Staff
24. *Scholastics Journal*
25. Pro Co, 23 September 1924, ISR.

CHAPTER FIVE

Promotions and the Burse

By the mid-1920s there were plenty of signs that the foreign missions were gradually but surely taking hold on the Irish people. The number of lay promoters of mission fundraising was rising steadily and they were communicating their enthusiasm to others. The regularly recurring preparation and distribution of the *Missionary Annals* led to the formation of a 'league' of lay helpers known as the Holy Ghost African Mission League, popularly called HGAML. The league depended on the annual contribution of one shilling or the life contribution of five shillings. A major annual enterprise of the League from the beginning was the Sale of Work held for many years at the Mansion House and later at other venues. The Sale of Work harnessed the faith, energy, goodwill and generosity of thousands of lay people and many organisations throughout the country. Zealous sisters from many convents sent large boxes of handiwork made by members of their community or by the school children under their charge. Promoters of the *Missionary Annals* sent parcels of goods from their subscribers and friends. Sewing and cookery classes provided splendid gifts.[1] Each year the league also organised a number of concerts, operatic and variety. Alicia Mann was the prime mover in organising them.

Another distinct organisation, the Burse, developed in 1932. One Michael O'Neill was its inspiration, a man to whom Irish Spiritans and the missions are greatly indebted. On a visit to Blackrock he learnt the needs of our missions and especially the need to support the students for the priesthood who were then living at the Castle and Willow Park. The well-founded legend is that Michael heard – correctly – how frugally the scholastics were living and wanted them to have 'rashers and eggs for breakfast', a wish that never materialised in that form. Michael was ably helped by Mick Morgan, a fellow Inchicore man. Austin Fennessy and John McAsey, both ordained later, were their Kimmage contacts.

---

1. MA, February 1931, p 36-7.

They organised a system whereby they secured promoters, each promoter being asked to procure ten members. Subscriptions were sixpence per month or three ha'pence per week, with the *Missionary Annals* distributed as a kind of receipt. This practice continued for decades and helped maintain students in Kimmage during those years when it received large members. The name 'Burse' refers to the sum of money needed to educate a student for the priesthood.

In 1948 the Holy Ghost African Mission League Missionary and the Burse were amalgamated and lay staff were employed, the first of whom was Kathleen Downey, now long retired but still helpfully involved in this centenary year 2011.[2]

For the next sixty years the Burse has been one of the principal sources of income for the upkeep of Kimmage and Spiritan Missions. While the name Burse is still often used and it has grown and developed over the years, the official name has changed to Promotions/Mission Animation. Under the leadership of Fr Jimmy Duggan and his team, the Burse developed new forms of fundraising such as the annual gymkhana in Kimmage which began in the early sixties and the Gala Day, a local event, initiated by Fr Paddy Cleary and Fr Michael Buckley, which provided great family fun and also, of course, raised much-needed funds.

The gymkhana had its origins in the fund-raising activities in the 1950s for the new school and chapel at St Mary's College. When the building committee in St Mary's ceased their activities the president, Charles Wilson, and his colleagues Leo and Brian Lea, Terry Sadlier, Stephen Lane and S. Baily transferred their expertise to raising funds for the Burse. Very quickly the gymkhana established itself as a major annual event for Kimmage attracting some of the great names in Irish show-jumping such as Iris Kellett, Diana Connolly Carew, Ned Campion, Jerry Mullen, Paul Darragh, Tommy Wade, Eddie Macken, Con Power, James Kiernan, Pat Doyle, Capt Hume Dudgeon and members of the army equestrian team. There were two arenas, one for senior and the other for junior competitors. As well as attracting great names in show-jumping, it attracted great crowds and provided

2. Myles Fay, 'Finances' in GTAN, p 309-11

splendid entertainment. The gymkhana soon became a feeder event at which competitors gained points for the Dublin Horse Show and soon developed into a two-day event held on a Saturday and Sunday. Sergeant-Major Stephen Hickey used to build the arena, helped by a member of the Committee, Terry Sadlier. The various events were sponsored by companies and firms throughout the country. No opportunity was lost for fund-raising so a Sale of Work was also organised with stalls just outside the railings of the enclosure yielding substantial income.

Promotions and the Sale of Work continued down to recent times to be the greatest source of income for the funding of Kimmage and its missions.[3] Mission Animation has been organised from 46 Lower Rathmines Road by a highly motivated team of lay people under the direction of one Spiritan. Each year the team promotes the work of missions and appeals for funds in a number of dioceses in Ireland allocated through the Irish Missionary Union. The Spiritan animation personnel then set out each weekend to different parishes where they usually received great hospitality from clergy and people. One confrère recalls visiting Cardinal Ó Fiaich in Armagh to report his presence to him. The first words of the cardinal were: 'Have you had your dinner yet?' They preached at all Masses on the weekend about the work of Spiritan missionaries and also about their financial needs. During the week they visited the schools within the parishes to promote the *Missionary Annals* and later *Outlook*. Outside of that they organised promotions groups within the parishes who continue to support the missions. On Pentecost Sunday each year the Promoters from all over the country are invited to Mass in Kimmage and to a meal afterwards. These were marvellous occasions in days gone by when very often 800 or 900 people showed up.[4]

The Sale of Work grew to a three-day event held in the Mansion House each year during December. It was especially welcome by the people of Dublin and elsewhere when times were lean. Great bargains were to be had especially in clothing

---

3. Fr Jimmy Duggan, Interview.
4. Fr Liam Martin, Interview.

and household goods. These goods were donated by generous benefactors, apostolic work societies, through the work of promoters and various factories and retail outlets throughout Ireland. A dedicated team of promoters acted as salespersons at the large number of stalls throughout the three days. They took responsibility for setting them up and setting out their wares and promoting sales. One of those remarkable people, Seán Treacy, helped for so many years in the preparation of the Sale of Work; now in his nineties, he still visits Kimmage weekly. Among the Spiritans who inspired and encouraged the work of the promoters and the organisers of the Sale of Work were Rev Philip Lynch and Brothers Killian Melligan and Matthias Connolly. There were raffles for a huge variety of hampers at the various stalls and the wheel of fortune was a great attraction offering very fine prizes. Overall it was a great social event with the same people turning up year after year and renewing old acquaintances over endless cups of tea and cake or scones of all varieties.

The Promotions Office also organised several major raffles throughout the year especially at Christmas time offering very attractive prices.

Great tribute must be paid to the long line of directors and their lay and Spiritan teams who engaged in this most difficult apostolate. Most of them look back on it as a great experience and with great joy at having met so many great and generous people without whom Kimmage and the missions could not have survived.

CHAPTER SIX

The Scholasticate Saga

Build or stop recruiting

On 1 September 1925 Fr Richard Hartnett was appointed Provincial Superior to succeed Fr Joseph Byrne who was promoted to the General Council. Like his predecessors, Fr Hartnett had been in the USA, where he was in charge of the Mission Band. The province was still in financial difficulties. Fr Hartnett was to bring his expertise in fundraising to bear on the major problem of finding accommodation for a rapidly expanding student population. The solution that was in place, as already noted, was only temporary.

The Generalate appointed six very able councillors to assist Fr Hartnett. These were, Fr Edward Crehan who had just completed his stint on the General Council; Fr Michael Meagher, a former missionary in Sierra Leone, founder of the Holy Ghost Missionary League and an experienced fund raiser; Fr Edward Leen a distinguished scholar, former Director of the House of Philosophy, a professor of ethics and psychology with two year's missionary experience and a growing reputation as a writer and educationalist; Fr Hugh Evans, novice master, and Fr Laurence Healy one of the veterans of the Province. The challenges they were facing were enormous.

One of the first acts of Fr Hartnett and his council was to reverse the decision of Fr Byrne regarding students attending university. At its first meeting in October 1925 it was decided that as many students as possible should be sent to UCD.[1] Afternoon tea for students, which had been discontinued as a cost-saving measure by Fr Byrne, was again allowed.

Although thoughts of building a senior scholasticate and novitiate in Kimmage surfaced frequently from the foundation of Kimmage, nothing really happened except for the extensions put up by John T. Murphy and Hugh Evans. Long before Fr Evans built the chapel and library, Fr Hartnett and his Council had serious discussions about erecting a senior scholasticate

---

1. Pro Co, 8 October 1925

with about 150 rooms at a cost of £30,000. It was decided to ask the Generalate for this money without interest with a promise to pay back the principal when possible. Fr Stafford, Provincial Bursar, was given the task of writing to Paris concerning all this in mid-September 1927.[2] Fr Stafford's letter did not provoke the desired response.

At this juncture there was a visitation of the Irish Province by the new Superior General, Archbishop Louis Le Hunsec, and Fr Joseph Byrne. From the point of view of vocations the situation in the Irish Province was looking good. Approximately 80 new members were professed in the previous five years, creating great hope for evangelisation in English-speaking missions. One of the major issues discussed with the visitors was that of allowing a large building exclusively for the scholasticate to be constructed at Kimmage. In December 1927, Fr Hartnett received a reply to their request. The General Council approved the construction, provided that the Province could afford it.[3]

By February 1928 there were proposals for getting new plans and new estimates for the building. The estimate presented in June 1928 for a building of 120 rooms was £30,000. Every possible means of fund-raising was explored. Plans and estimates for the novitiate were passed unanimously.[4] By September plans for the scholasticate were ready for inspection and explanations were available.[5] The new wing to the novitiate was approved by the Generalate in December 1928. Kimmage as a site for the scholasticate was also approved. Permission to build the scholasticate, however, would only be given when half the money was on hand.[6] Pressure to build increased when the number of novices rose to twenty-six in August 1929. There was now an absolute necessity to build or stop recruiting. That was the message coming from the Provincialate.[7] Although money had begun to come in, the target had not yet been reached.

2. Pro Co, 11 Sept and 27 Sept. 1927
3. Pro Co, 26 Dec 1927
4. Pro Co, 28 June-1 July 1928
5. Pro Co, 22 September 1928
6. Pro Co, 23 December 1928
7. Pro Co, 30 June 1929

57

Between January and June 1929 a total of £5,700 was received from various sources.

The proposal received a severe shock in June 1930 when the General Council proposed that the senior scholasticate should be in Willow Park. It was like sending the whole project back to the drawing board, and it caused endless delays and no small amount of acrimony. Why this sudden and unilateral reversal? It seems that some Spiritan bishops along with some distinguished laymen were against building in Kimmage. This created a division among the Provincial Councillors some of whom wanted the building in Willow Park while others wanted it in Kimmage. To add to the confusion, the General Council suggested that two wings should be added to the Castle in Blackrock which would then be used exclusively as a scholasticate. Fr Hartnett and his Council were unanimous in opposing this suggestion while the Blackrock community was opposed to building in either Willow Park or at the Castle. Any such move would be prejudicial to both the senior scholasticate and to the school at Blackrock.[8]

In August 1931 the project of building a senior scholasticate was postponed for twelve months until the Superior General came on visitation. When Archbishop Le Hunsec came to Ireland for the Eucharistic Congress in 1932 his stay was very short, and there was no change in the situation.

Meanwhile the number of aspirants increased rapidly. In the autumn of 1931 twenty novices were professed and were destined for Willow Park to add to the already crowded situation there. The intake to the novitiate increased to 37 in 1932-3, and that same year the total number studying philosophy and theology at Blackrock came to one hundred and thirty-two.[9]

To remedy the situation it was decided to move the novitiate away from Kimmage. A number of possible locations were considered. Eventually the Province bought Kilshane House between Bansha and Tipperary Town, having secured the permission of Archbishop Harty. The property was bought for £12,000, the money for which came from the scholasticate 'Building

8. Pro Co, 8 April, 13 June, 13 September, 13 October 1931
9. BG, 35, p 983

Fund' set up by Fr Hartnett in 1928. The novitiate opened in
Kilshane in November 1933 with Fr John J. McCarthy as novice
master and Fr Hugh Evans as Superior. There were thirty-five
novices, thirty two from Spiritan juniorates and colleges and
three from Christian Brothers' schools. Not only was there a
change in location, there was a huge change in the process of
formation.

Theologians return to Kimmage 1933
The theology students at the Castle returned to Kimmage in
November 1933 with Fr John Kearney still as Director. The other
members of staff were, Fr James Murphy, Fr Bernard Fennelly
and Fr Michael Kennedy, who was still Director of Philosophers
and lived in Blackrock. Brother Dismas, who had been transferred to Blackrock in 1916, now returned to take care of the
kitchen and catering. Fr Nicholas O'Loughlin, a veteran fund-
raiser with the Irish Mission Band in the USA, was specially
asked for to be Community Superior and Director of the Holy
Ghost African Mission League.[10] A better choice could hardly be
found; he was a tireless worker and his contribution to
Kimmage was enormous.

The arrival of the theology students in November 1933
brought a whole new surge of energy and zeal for self-help projects to the Kimmage campus. Gone were the croquet lawns and
the mild football games played by the novices. Playing fields,
new walks, flower beds and rockeries were arranged. The little
river Poddle which flows through the grounds was dammed to
make a swimming pool for the summer of 1934. Hurling and
football matches were resumed and challenges sent between the
philosophers in Blackrock and the theologians in Kimmage.[11]
Space for indoor games in Kimmage was non-existent, so the
students cleared out an old barn in the farmyard which they
then used for indoor games and recreation.[12]

That September the National Missionary Exhibition in the
Mansion House attracted great crowds over a period of three

10. Pro Co, 23 September 1933
11. E. Ryan, notes
12. Scholastics Journal

weeks. 'The period of the Exhibition was a busy one for the scholastics, for whom the work at the Mansion House was a labour of love, dear to all who are labouring at or preparing to spread the gospel in pagan lands. Each day we went down in relays to relieve one another and for the most part the journeys to and fro were negotiated by the pony and trap'.[13]

The programme of studies in the theologate varied little from what it had been in 1924. A very small number of students were sent for studies in the Gregorian University in Rome. That policy was to change when the decision was taken in 1927 to send six or eight students each year after philosophy to study theology in Rome, France or Germany.[14] This was a further reversal of the stringent policy of Fr Byrne.

In spite of the rapid growth in numbers, the building of the scholasticate was still postponed. Early in 1933, Fr Lena from the General Council was still pushing the idea of building around the Castle in Blackrock. A memorandum was drawn up by the senior scholasticate staff stating in the clearest possible terms why Blackrock was most unsuitable for a permanent house of studies. Fr John Kearney, Fr James Murphy and Fr Bernard Fennelly signed this memorandum.[15] Certain members of the Provincial Council were convinced that the General Council in Paris had no understanding of the facts. The disagreement between the Provincial Council and the Generalate worsened during the first half of 1934 as the Generalate refused to accept the objections about the unsuitability of Blackrock.

Fr Hartnett and his council were now almost at their wits' end trying to cope with an almost impossible situation. A special meeting of the Provincial Council to deal with the situation, attended by all the Councillors and the staff of Kimmage and the Castle along with the bursar of Blackrock College was held on 30 April 1934. The plans for the senior scholasticate in Kimmage were discussed in detail. All present were agreed that this was a question of the most urgent necessity – they had to build at once if they were going to house the ever-growing number of aspirants.

13. MA, November 1934, p 222, *Kimmage Diary*
14. Pro Co, 3 July 1927
15. Pro Co, 20 February 1933

The plan adopted was for a building with 160 bedrooms, study hall, classrooms, dining room and large chapel. The estimated cost was between £35,000 and £40,000. The building fund, which had been depleted by the purchase of Kilshane, stood at just £10,000; a further £30,000 was needed to build. It was agreed to approach the Generalate for a loan of £30,000 to be repaid in instalments. Fr Hartnett asked the colleges to help by paying the interest on the proposed loan. He pleaded with Mgr Le Hunsec to respond positively to their request. The response when it came was a strong negative. There was no loan forthcoming and Mgr Le Hunsec was adamant that there would be no reversal of the decision to have the scholasticate at Blackrock as is evident from his letter to Fr Hartnett of 13 June 1934.[16]

The reply of Fr Hartnett and his Councillors show how deeply hurt they were by Mgr Le Hunsec's letter. They felt he had misunderstood completely the whole reason why the Province continued to maintain the colleges. They were needed as a source of vocations and as a source of income. Personnel who were trained in Spiritan Colleges, too, best met the educational needs of the missions. The greatest hurt, however, came from having the unanimous decision of the Provincial Council of the Irish Province and the Councils of Blackrock College and the senior scholasticate treated as being more specious than real, as having no basis. In spite of their hurt, they were reluctant to believe that the Mother House was willing to treat them as lacking in a common honesty of purpose. Fr Hartnett and his Council continued their firm opposition to building at Blackrock, and supported once more the memorandum of the senior scholasticate staff. Even Rome, they claimed, could not fail to accept its arguments that religious discipline and studies were, and would continue to be, damaged by proximity to Blackrock College. All the members of the Provincial Council signed this letter written on 21 June 1934 which shows in the strongest possible terms their unanimous opposition to the proposals of the Mother House to build at Blackrock or at Willow Park.[17]

Mgr Le Hunsec's intransigence on this matter was almost

---

16. IPA, Le Hunsec to Hartnett
17. IPA, Kimmage Box 1

certainly due to the very strong influence of Fr Joseph Byrne, the Irish member of the General Council. This can be seen from the correspondence between Fr Hartnett and Fr Byrne in 1927 when Fr Hartnett wrote a memorandum justifying the existence of the colleges on the grounds that they provided vocations and financial support for the scholasticate.[18] Fr Byrne wrote a scathing response of about 3,000 words in which he portrayed the colleges as obstacles to the Congregation's work since they catered for the rich and prosperous. Far from supporting the junior scholasticates, they were a hindrance to those who were fund-raising who had to try and distance themselves from the colleges, so that they would not be perceived as part of the same establishment. The argument that the colleges and juniorates provided vocations, he maintained, did not hold up. Between 1860 and 1926 the College Scholasticate system had provided 196 priests. Of these, 66 were dead in 1927. Of the 130 Irish Spiritans alive in 1927, a total of 61 were in Europe, 25 in the USA, 14 in Trinidad, and 30, including 6 bishops, were in Africa. The SMAs, who had no second level colleges, sent 10 priests to Africa in 1927. The Columbans founded in 1918 but with no secondary schools or juniorates had 100 priests and 100 seminarians in 1927. Mill Hill sent 24 missionaries to the missions in 1927. 'If the efforts made by the Fathers in Ireland were made in Sierra Leone, Nigeria or East Africa, there would have been marvellous results and there would be an indigenous clergy without too long to wait.' And as for financial support, he wrote: 'One can count more on charity than on our colleges. Proof: £34,000 in burses. No need to insist.' This response was written for Mgr Le Hunsec and certainly influenced his dealings with Ireland thereafter.[19]

Under Way at Last with Dr Dan Murphy

A number of important changes occurred in 1933 and 1934 that would profoundly affect the development of Kimmage and its phenomenal growth as a missionary college. In 1933 Fr Joseph Byrne was nominated to succeed Bishop Henry Gogarty as Vicar Apostolic of Kilimanjaro and ordained bishop in Rockwell on 19 March 1933. Fr Francis Griffin who had administered the

18. IPA, Memorandum, 29 September 1927
19. IPA, Byrne to Le Hunsec, December 1927

vicariate of Kilimanjaro after the death of Bishop Gogarty was elected to the General Council in June 1933 and took up office in Paris in March 1934. Later that year, the man who would lead Kimmage and the Irish Province forward as a missionary-sending society, Dr Dan Murphy, was appointed Provincial. He held his first Council meeting on 29 August 1934.

At that first meeting the Council made a number of far-reaching decisions regarding studies. As many students as possible should be sent to university for a pass or honours degree according to their abilities in view of the needs of the missions. The Irish language should be studied more seriously in the colleges and scholasticates. Both Irish and French should be introduced into the curriculum of the senior scholasticate. The most important step taken was to implement a decision of the previous Council to send academically gifted students to Rome, Fribourg or Louvain to study for licentiates and doctorates in theology.[20] For financial reasons very few students were sent to Rome before this time and those who went resided at the French seminary while studying at the Gregorian University or the Angelicum.

Dr Murphy continued the policy of Fr Hartnett with regard to having the senior scholasticate buildings at Kimmage. In December, 1934 Fr Francis Griffin, from the General Council, visited Ireland and attended a meeting of the Provincial Council on 18 December. At this meeting it was unanimously agreed to build the senior scholasticate in Kimmage. The building was to be done in stages depending on the availability of funds. They estimated that the building without the chapel would cost about £30,000. They had £15,000 on hand and sought authorisation to raise a loan of £15,000 at 2%. The Mother House was to be requested to remit, for at least five years, the personal contribution of the Irish Fathers in favour of the Province.[21] In April, 1935, the General Council finally agreed in principle for the second time to have the buildings in Kimmage, but no work was to begin until Fr Griffin had made an official visitation. On 21 May 1935, the General Council approved the new plans for Kimmage.

20. Pro Co, 29 August 1934
21. Pro Co, 18 December 1934

A building committee was formed to assist Fr Stafford, the Provincial Bursar, with this onerous task. The chairperson was Fr John Charles (later Archbishop) McQuaid; the other members were Fr E. Leen, Fr J. Kearney, Fr M. Kennedy, Fr D Fahey, Fr N. O'Loughlin and Fr Jim Burke. The building itself was designed principally by Fr Burke, bursar in Kimmage, (1934-35), with the advice of Fr Kearney. The architects were Messrs Jones and Kelly. By the end of 1935 the Provincial Council, with the help of the building committee and the architects, was able to submit a detailed memorandum to the Mother House. This gave facts and figures about student numbers, accommodation and costs of building with a breakdown of the money available.

At this stage the new building was designed to accommodate 160 students. The existing building in Kimmage could house 40. The number of novices in Kilshane that year was 43, double the average number of previous years. New estimates were also given showing that the cost would be between £55,000 and £60,000. Funds in the Province for building had risen from around £9,000 in February 1934 to about £24,000 in December 1935. More than £15,000 had been contributed in one year and nine months. The Provincial Council requested the Mother House to approach the Sacred Congregation of Religious in Rome to obtain consent to raise a loan of £35,000. The members were convinced that they could repay it at the rate of £5,000 per year given the financial state of the Province.

At last, in 1936, the building project got under way. Rome sanctioned the borrowing of £35,000 and the Provincial Procurator was authorised to go ahead in April 1936. The tenders from contractors were opened on Monday 4 May. The tender of an old established firm, Messrs Maher and Murphy, for £46,543 was accepted for a building in concrete.

Mass concrete was cheaper than building with pointed stone; it was also quicker and this was very desirable in the circumstances. It wasn't a very favourable time for building as there was a worldwide economic depression and an economic war raged between England and Ireland. The people were poor, but the missionary spirit was flourishing and generous promoters provided funds. The money was spent carefully and the simple style, the modest doorways and windows, the small rooms with low ceilings reflected the standards accepted in those years.[22]

Fr Nicholas O'Loughlin, the superior of Kimmage and director of the Holy Ghost Missionary League, did inestimable work in fundraising and in keeping this major undertaking before the minds of the people through the *Missionary Annals*. Through Fr O'Loughlin a very large number of people donated £120, the cost of a room. Fr Hartnett had introduced this scheme in 1928. The spiritual side of the whole project was kept to the forefront and meetings were organised by promoters in the homes of friends, along the lines of the Legion of Mary with readings and exhortations. Promoters were forthcoming and they collected sixpence per month from the members of their circles. It was a further means of promoting the *Missionary Annals*. Dr Dan Murphy also circularised the provincial newspapers and arranged with them that they would from time to time publish articles on the missions. The articles were written in Kimmage under the direction of Fr Michael Kennedy, and six or seven were sent for publication in the provincial newspapers each week. There was always a concealed appeal for financial help. Several fathers were detailed to show films and give talks on the missions, and indirectly at least, to refer to the necessity of financing the proposed building of a new house of studies. Many other sources of revenue were tapped – not all with pronounced success.[23]

The whole scheme caused much excitement and was a great topic of conversation. The scholastics, enlightened by rumour and gossip claimed that Fr McQuaid was leader of 'the good-architecture group' while Fr John Kearney spoke for 'the save-the-expense school'.[24] A cursory reading of the minutes of the building committee convinces one that the scholastics must have had a mole at the meetings.

The site of the building was determined[25] after careful consideration. Finally, it was decided to build on a large cow pas-

22. E. Ryan, Notes
23. IPA Short History, p 5. This short history seems to have been a summary by the building committee.
24. E Ryan
25. IPA, Minutes of Building Committee Meetings, Kimmage Box 2, hereafter BCM

ture to the south of the Manor building, and which a stream, hedge and ornamental trees separated from the croquet lawn. The new building would be connected with the old one by a corridor (The Venerable Libermann Corridor) which entered at the south-east corner; a portion of it can still be seen there, forming part of a rear entrance. Older confrères will remember the 'surplice presses' in this corridor, and the absence of windows in a portion of it. These features arose from the original intention to build the chapel in the quadrangle between the Manor and the new scholasticate building with proposed access to it from the Venerable Libermann Corridor.

Initially the new building was designed for the theology students only. Philosophy students were to occupy the old building and the chapel was to be mid-way between the two faculties. The original plan was for two wings with a connecting corridor which would run by the superior's office and the classrooms. The two wings were to be three storeys high, while the connecting corridor was to be just two storeys. The greater part of the space above the corridor was to be an open dormitory with a few rooms at each end for the director and bursar. This portion was also to have a flat roof, to which a third storey might be added later on. Such was the original plan when Bishop John Neville turned the first sod in the field towards the southern end of the west wing in June 1936. The work had at last begun and a great sigh of relief was heard, so it was said. Lorries by the dozen brought sand and gravel from Kill, Co. Kildare. Soon the site became a sea of wooden casings and poles, clearly visible from the Hell Fire Club.[26]

The connecting corridor between the Manor House and the new building was first built and roofed. On Sunday, 25 October 1936, the Feast of Christ the King, the foundation stone was laid by his Excellency, Mgr Paschal Robinson, and the Papal Nuncio. Fr McQuaid composed the inscription in Latin on the stone in the front quadrangle.

Progress on the building was delayed for about six months by the Builders' Labourers' Strike which began in the Spring of 1937. Part of the house had been roofed already. During this

---

26. IPA, *Short History*, pp 7-8

respite the whole scheme was reconsidered and the decision was taken to add the third storey to the building between the two main wings, thus making provision for about 30 extra rooms. This change had been considered as far back as October 1936, as numbers were increasing rapidly.[27]

In what can only be described as an extraordinary feat of organisation a mammoth crowd of 12,000 members of The Burse gathered at Kimmage for the Feast of the Assumption of Our Blessed Lady on 15 August 1937. The grounds south of the scholasticate building (uncompleted) were the point of assembly and here sections had been marked off and assigned to each unit group. The organisation of this mighty throng was the responsibility of Commandant Buggle and his assistants. The first events included a long procession with a statue of Our Lady carried by four bearers starting from the Old House and making its way to the rear or south of the new and incomplete building. The procession was led by the No. 1 Army Band followed by the Kimmage choir, detachments from the Catholic Boy Scouts and the clergy led by Bishop Neville. Finally came Bishop Shanahan who gave Benediction of the Blessed Sacrament from the south corridor of the new building. This was followed by an address of welcome by Fr Murphy who expressed his pleasure that the Students Burse members were the first guests to be officially welcomed in the new House of Studies. 'So vast a gathering of missionary co-operators, he stressed, mirrored the great movement in the church which was gathering such a great harvest of souls into the Divine Granaries. Fr E Leen gave a talk on the Holy Spirit. Fr Fred Fullen, Director of the Student Burse said the occasion was used so that the Congregation could express its gratitude to the promoters and their helpers for the work they were doing in supporting the missions.'

To feed this mighty crowd, field kitchens were everywhere. Buffet-tables had been arranged in the future dining room, study hall and corridors, while in the adjoining field two huge marquees were ready to receive visitors. There were fires of all sorts from gas burners to the humble wood fire all bubbling with cauldrons and boilers of all shapes and sizes. The matter-of-fact miracle of feeding 12,000 was accomplished by the efforts

27. BCM

of some 400 women helpers.[28]

Around this time, due to an intervention of Fr Michael Kennedy, it was decided to change the site chosen for the chapel and to locate it where it now stands. There was major revision of the plans including the addition of the two transepts and the tower. On 2 February 1938, the foundation stone of the chapel was blessed and placed on the gospel side (the left-hand side as one faces the altar) of the sanctuary by Bishop Neville. There was a celebration for the members of the congregation, who were entertained to lunch again in the connecting corridor. Work on the chapel was to begin in May 1938, but it was delayed because of the building strike.

The first wing of the scholasticate was completed in 1937 and the whole building, except for the chapel, was ready for the following September. During the summer of 1938 the philosophers from Blackrock began to transfer their property to Kimmage. A general inventory was made of all the goods belonging to the scholasticate which could be legitimately carried off to Kimmage. Groups of students were sent over to Kimmage at short notice to begin work on laying out temporary recreation grounds. Indoors, the students had the task of cleaning and polishing the rooms and corridors. Then on 29 August 1938, the philosophy students took up residence in Kimmage in the west wing of the new building, which was then the wing nearest the original farmyard. Around the same time the Burse team came from Blackrock to take up residence in the old house which had been reorganised and redecorated. The members of the Burse team were Fr Fred Fullen, Fr Joe Carter and Fr Paddy Nolan. Fr Joe Horgan, Fr Bertie Farrell and Fr Ned Ryan were engaged in promoting the work of the missions.

As the new chapel was far from complete the theologians' study in the east wing was used as a temporary chapel. The philosophers' study upstairs was given to the theologians, while three new classrooms were assigned as temporary study halls to the philosophers. All staff, philosophers and theologians shared the spacious new dining room.

The day fixed for the official opening and blessing was Sunday 30 October, the Feast of Christ the King. An immense

28. BCM

amount of work was put into the preparation by the students who laid the foundations for having the whole area between the Manor House and chapel tarmacadamised, thus overcoming that ancient enemy of Kimmage – mud.

The ceremony of blessing was performed by the Superior General, Archbishop Le Hunsec. It was presided over by the Papal Nuncio. There were six other bishops present along with many distinguished lay persons including the Taoiseach, Éamon de Valera. Following the ceremony the guests were entertained to lunch in the new dining room, while the students dined in the theologians' study hall.[29]

It was not until Sunday 18 December, however, that the new chapel began to be used for all community exercises, and it would be a couple of years before the chapel was completely finished. The decoration and installation of permanent furnishings was a slow process. All the oak timber for the seating and parquet floors came from Kilshane farm. The high altar, the altars in the transepts, the precious stones in the tabernacle and many of the stained glass windows were gifts received by Fr Leen. Fr Phil O'Shea gave the Holy Cross altar, Fr Evans that of St Joseph. Most of the side altars and the other gifts came through Fr O'Loughlin. The Holy Ghost African Mission League, under his direction, supplied all the altar linen and vestments for the church and procured bed linen and made up hundreds of sheets.[30]

Mr Gunning designed the sanctuary lamp in bronze. The simple yet very beautiful Stations of the Cross were done in the new medium of opal glass. This type of glass is not stained but the colours are burned into it, giving a suggestion of brilliancy. The organ in the choir gallery came from Rathmines church. During the rebuilding of that church after the burning of 1920, a new organ was installed. Canon Fleming, the parish priest, gave the old organ to Kimmage. Fr Kearney supervised its installation, which was done by a Mr Abel. Fr Kearney would not allow a sixteen-foot pipe to be added, maintaining that the function of the organ was to accompany the plain chant. Towards

29. *Provincial Bulletin*, (PB) January 1939, pp 13-18
30. IPA, *Short History*, p 6

the end of his life he relented and in time a pipe was added.[31]

The impressive stained glass windows are, with two exceptions, the work of Mr W. Dowling of Harry Clarke studios. The other two windows are by the Earley Studios (St John) and Mr McGoldrick of the Túr Gloine Studios (St Colmcille), this latter window being one of the finest and most remarkable of all the windows. The windows along the side aisles are beautiful full-figure depictions of the patron saints of the altars.

When the scholasticate and chapel were completed in 1942 there was no debt. Vocations, however, continued to increase at an unprecedented rate, due in large measure to the very significant increase in the number of novices coming from Spiritan colleges and the increase in numbers coming from other secondary schools as a result of the inspiring talks given by Fr Bertie Farrell, the Vocations Director. This led to a demand for further accommodation. In 1941 a study hall was built for the philosophers along with a fairly substantial two-storey building for the lay staff. Final plans for a new wing were passed in December, 1945. Messrs Jones and Kelly were again the architects, and the builders whose tender was accepted were Messrs Maher and Murphy. Their tender was for £21,159. The new wing, known as the Sacred Heart wing, provided sleeping quarters for ninety students. This wing consisted of two storeys added to the already existing study hall and library. The study hall had a beautiful parquet floor and had three very fine stained glass windows at the south end. These stained glass windows were removed before the building was sold to Telecom Éireann. One of them, depicting Our Lady Seat of Wisdom, forms the large window of the Shanahan House oratory.

For a short time in 1945 and 1946 some philosophers had to be housed again in the Old Novitiate. Shortage of space was so acute that portions of the new wing were being occupied before it was completed. Students gained access to the middle corridor not from the stairs but from the flat roof of the toilets and showers in the dressing room area. Although the rooms were being occupied there was no central heating during the winter of 1946.

To make room for all the buildings, the original farmyard

31. IPA, *Short History*, pp 9-10

had to be demolished. A new farmyard was begun about 1937. At the same time consideration was given to building a new swimming pool. This coincided with the scheme of Dublin Corporation to keep the Poddle from flooding. The Poddle waters could be controlled by a sluice gate at Firhouse and flood waters could be directed to the Dodder. At the upper end of Kimmage property, however, the Tymon river flowed into the Poddle. The water from this river could not be controlled, and this was the principal cause of flooding around Mount Argus and the lower stretch of the Poddle. Dublin Corporation constructed a large culvert across Kimmage farm through Mrs Margaret Doherty's adjoining farm, down to Terenure College and from there back to the Dodder through Bushy Park. From the same point of confluence of the Poddle and Tymon there was an ancient stream known as Deane's Watercourse which provided water to Kimmage lands, Mrs Doherty's lands and Terenure College. As the deeds clearly indicate, this watercourse went back to the days when Joseph Deane lived in Terenure House. It was from this stream that water was taken for the swimming pool.

For a time it seemed as if the Corporation would object. As all the groups mentioned had water rights going back to the eighteenth century the Corporation could not interfere. After a certain amount of negotiation with the Corporation authorities and meetings with the city engineers and law agents an amicable solution was reached. The Corporation agreed to put in the floor and build the retaining walls and supply the piping and sluice gate of the swimming pool, if the excavations were undertaken by Kimmage. Students carried out some of the excavation, but the work was very heavy, especially as they went lower down. Messrs Maher and Murphy, most kindly and without any remuneration, put about 20 of their employees on the job for about a fortnight, and so the swimming pool was built with no expense to Kimmage. For many years it provided a very valuable facility to the students and staff, even if the water was not always the purest.

CHAPTER SEVEN

Life in the new seminary

All these building programmes were with a view to providing accommodation and training for future missionaries. Let us now go back: before any new buildings were approved of or begun the students of theology from Blackrock had moved into Kimmage in November 1933. The novices had departed for Kilshane and the novitiate house became the house of studies for the theology students. The philosophy students, however, had to remain in Blackrock as Kimmage could not accommodate them. Fr John Kearney was still Director and Superior and would remain in the latter role until Fr O'Loughlin was able to take up that office. Fr Cleary remained bursar in Kimmage until Fr Kennedy was appointed to replace him. For Fr Bernard Fr Fennelly and Fr James Murphy these changes were a great relief since they no longer needed to commute to Blackrock; the students had come to them. But two other professors, Frs Michael Kennedy and Denis Fahey now had to commute from Blackrock to Kimmage. As well as being Director of Philosophers in Blackrock, Fr Kennedy was also Professor of Moral Theology at Kimmage. Eventually in 1935 Fr Kennedy came to reside in Kimmage to be more closely associated with the theologians as professor and as bursar of the community. Fr Fahey was Professor of Philosophy in Blackrock and professor of Church History at Kimmage.[1]

The fact that Fr Kearney was still Director of Theologians made it easier for those making the transition to Kimmage. He was a saintly man, and had a profound and formative influence not just on the students and community but on the province as a whole. His advice was sought and followed in many things such as the launching and production of the *Missionary Annals*, the *Holy Ghost Hymnal* and the nomination of candidates to the post of Vicar Apostolic as well as the planning of the new scholasticate. He always insisted on maintaining the highest standards – he was thought by some to be too austere and restrictive.

---

1. E. Ryan, Notes, ISR

Though he was never personally on the overseas missions, he was eminently pastoral and missionary in his outlook. After 19 years he retired as Director in 1937 but remained on the staff as spiritual director and Professor of Pastoral Theology. The post of Director of Theology was filled by Fr Pat O'Carroll, fresh from Rome with a Doctorate in Divinity. Fr O'Carroll was appointed Professor of Moral Theology and also taught liturgy. His appointment helped to infuse a welcome note of humanity into the house because of his youth and infectious good humour.

As already noted the philosophy students and staff came to Kimmage in August of 1938 raising the total number of students in Kimmage to 177. Their Director was Fr Jack Dempsey who had been appointed to that post four years earlier on completing his doctorate in the Gregorian University. As soon as he arrived in Kimmage he was entrusted with the duties of bursar of the senior scholasticate, thereby joining that galaxy of doctors of theology who were called on in the Congregation to turn their minds to more earthly matters. A year later he was appointed to the Provincial Council, but died suddenly in his sleep on 2 January 1940 while in Bundoran to give a convent retreat.[2] Fr Bernard J. Kelly who had recently returned from Fribourg took over as Director of Philosophy in July 1939. At this time it was also announced that Fr Edward Leen had been appointed Superior of Kimmage to succeed Fr O'Loughlin while continuing his duties as Professor of Ethics and Psychology in the House of Philosophy.

At a very early age Fr Kelly found himself in a very challenging office as Director of an ever-increasing number of students, many of whom were attending university. Altogether, after receiving 34 newly professed members in September 1939, there were 80 students in the House of Philosophy.[3] Fr Kelly taught part of the philosophy course and later taught patrology and homiletics to the theology students. As Director of Music, he trained an excellent choir which was called on from time to time to broadcast Masses on Raidió Éireann. As Director of Philosophy he was highly rated for his approachability, his bal-

2. PB, vol 2, no 2, pp 91-92 April 1940
3. PB vol 2, no.1, 16-17 January 1940

anced judgement and fairness. Although junior in years he had
no hesitation in taking a firm stand against what he considered
unhelpful interventions by senior members of staff such as Fr
Fahey and Fr Leen. As a great lover of all things Gaelic, he did
much to promote the Irish language among the students and
even composed some theological works in Irish as well as several books and many articles on spiritual and theological matters
in English. Many of his former students would consider him one
the brightest lights to have graced the Irish Spiritan Province.

Kimmage now had an excellent community and staff to lead
it towards the future. The superior, Fr Leen, had immense
experience as Director of Philosophy in 1917, as missionary with
Bishop Shanahan in Nigeria, as headmaster of Blackrock
College, as lecturer, writer and retreat-giver. Through his writings he was already recognised at home and abroad as an
authority on Christian spirituality. The houses of study were at
this time led by two bright young men in Fr O'Carroll and Fr
Kelly who over the years would give sterling service to their respective tasks.

The completion of the new senior scholasticate buildings
saw the realisation of the dreams of several generations of Irish
Spiritans. It was a tribute to the zeal and energy of successive
provincial superiors who helped to realise this dream. The new
house of studies also represented the faith and generosity of the
Irish people who were unfailing in their support of the missionary cause. For many decades Holy Ghost Missionary College,
Kimmage became a household name throughout the country.
Kimmage and mission were one and the same. Kimmage became part of the greatest missionary movement that Ireland has
ever experienced, in due course becoming home of the largest
missionary-sending body in the country.

The majority of missionaries from the Irish Province did all
their post-novitiate studies in Kimmage. As most of the buildings, grounds and other facilities and amenities have now gone,
it is important to try and recapture some of the spirit and atmosphere of Kimmage, which was the training centre for hundreds
of missionaries for many decades.

The facilities were considered adequate for the time. The
bedrooms were simple and furniture was very basic. The win-

dows were narrow with frosted glass, the colours were dull and
the overall appearance had a depressing effect. Each room had a
bed, a table with a book-shelf attached, a wardrobe and a wash-
stand complete with basin and jug. They did not have running
water. All rooms and corridors had central heating and the
bathrooms had hot and cold water. The large study halls for the
philosophy and theology students were well lighted; bedrooms,
however, were only supplied with 40-watt bulbs. The very spacious dining room served the teaching staff and students, but
the other members of the community such as the Provincial
team, the Burse team and the brothers had separate dining
rooms. At the end of the students' dining room furthest from the
kitchen there was a pulpit complete with microphone from
which students read during meals. Theology students preached
homilies during breakfast, after which they had to report to the
director for his comments on content and performance. Some
more daring and flamboyant students would enliven an otherwise dull breakfast with a few hilarious remarks, some of which
have passed into Congregation folklore. There was an unforget-
table morning when a student preacher began in a deep low
voice with: 'To hell with the Pope', which he repeated three
times, each time in a louder voice. Startled staff and students
who didn't know his flair for drama thought he was going mad.
Then he announced quite soberly that that was what they were
saying in the Kremlin.

Brother Dismas and lay helpers worked untiringly in the
kitchen for long hours cooking for all categories in the community and for guests. Students helped with the serving of meals
and with the washing up. The diet was reasonably good even
from the earliest days. All got three meals and two snacks a day.
In later times students were deprived of the morning snack,
probably because of the war. Meals were eaten in silence while a
student read from a book selected by the director. Many found
the food inadequate at times. A few verses of scripture were
read at the beginning of each meal and at the end of lunch the
martyrology, giving details of martyrs and saints whose feasts
or anniversaries would occur on the following day, was read in
Latin.

In the years following the completion of the scholasticate

buildings, students from both faculties spent a great deal of time laying out their own recreation grounds. Gradually they made roads and pathways throughout the grounds. The students of the theology faculty were aided in their work by a donkey called 'Harry', who was used to draw stones and sand from long distances. He even merited most of an article in the *Missionary Annals* for his labours, and for his abilities to outwit the scholastics with his stubbornness.[4] Lawns were laid out and trees, shrubs and flowers were planted. Playing pitches were prepared for Gaelic football, hurling, rugby and soccer. Games became a major feature of outdoor recreation in Kimmage. Annual leagues in all sports, in which most students took part, were organised. Some of the highlights of the year were the inter-faculty matches in all codes but especially in Gaelic football and rugby. These inter-faculty matches were fiercely competitive. In Gaelic football and rugby victory usually went to the weightier and wilier theologians, but in soccer the more agile philosophers were often the victors. Kimmage rugby gained a 'reputation' from visiting teams for 'its exceptionally robust' quality. One former student of the late 1940s recalls one of those fiercely competitive inter-faculty rugby games: 'I remember one occasion when a senior member of the theology team, a winger of some repute since his school days, was floored by a heel tap when in full flight for the line. His verbal reaction left scorch marks on the grass, which would not be of any consequence, except, on this occasion, he was right at the feet of the Director of Theologians. It is unknown if there were any 'consequences'. He went on to serve many long years in Africa'.[5] As regards physical needs and physical exercise students were well catered for. There was a great tradition of the long walk, going back to the very beginning of Kimmage among the novices but especially among the senior scholastics. Students were known to set out on a mid-winter morning after an early Mass and breakfast to head out over Kippure for Mullaghcleevaun reciting morning prayer and doing their meditation on the way. No matter how tired and battered they were on returning, it was a point of honour to

4. T. Roche, Notes
5. P. Heeran, *Kilshane to Kimmage*, unpublished memoir

be in one's place next morning kneeling erect for morning prayer.

Outings to the scouts' den in Larch Hill were part of the Christmas and Easter break periods. These were great occasions when students from both houses organised their respective events, consisting of a full meal prepared in Kimmage kitchen and transported sometimes by horse and cart, but mostly by students themselves in haversacks. The day usually finished with a hilarious concert, free-for-all singing, at which hidden talent of all sorts was discovered. The weeks of summer were punctuated with outing to the seaside, Portmarnock being the resort of choice. Students cycled there, carrying food in haversacks on their backs. The food was then prepared by a group appointed to cater beforehand. Assured of a good meal, the rest could settle into a day of swimming, football, walking or a quiet read. In earlier times, food and utensils were transported by horse and cart. On one occasion the horse bolted in Portmarnock breaking the traces and wrecking the harness. That evening two students pushed the cart from Portmarnock across Dublin city to Kimmage, while another student rode the horse home in comfort.

A wide variety of indoor entertainment became available to the students. There were facilities for games such as table tennis, snooker, darts and badminton. There was a strong tradition of music in both faculties and it was customary to have music recitals on winter evenings especially in the house of philosophy. The Kimmage orchestra under the direction of a theology student helped not only to provide entertainment for the students but also helped to develop the musical talents of many students. Soirées, concerts and plays featured very much around Christmas and the New Year. There was an abundance of talent available and students were encouraged to develop those talents.

The musical tradition in Kimmage went back to the earliest days and especially to Fr Evans. When Fr Evans departed for Kilshane in 1933 the tradition was continued by Fr Michael Kennedy, who, as a student had taken an active part in the Sistine Choir in Rome where he perfected his knowledge of and proficiency in polyphonic singing and plain chant. Successive choir directors, namely, Fr Bernard J. Kelly, Fr Pearse Moloncy and Fr John Chisholm, maintained the high standards achieved by Fr Kennedy. Kimmage choir made history when it made its first broadcast over Raidió Éireann during Advent, 1936. A tradition developed that the Advent Sunday Masses and the Christmas midnight and morning Masses each year were broadcast by Raidió Éireann from Kimmage. Kimmage Gaelic Choir made history in December 1959 when it began the first of five broadcasts from Raidió Éireann of a repertoire of ancient Gaelic and some Latin hymns which had not been heard for centuries. This had been the fruit of the intense work of Fr John Chisholm who through his research rediscovered a great collection of Irish hymns which had been lost when the Irish language ceased to be widely spoken. The choir was accompanied by the harpist Sheila Cuthbert and they received wide acclaim in the press. 'The Gaelic Choir, in five broadcasts from Raidió Éireann has given a new sound to hymn singing, and a new hope to choirmasters and teachers throughout the country'.[6]

Studies in the New Scholasticate
Students arriving in Kimmage from the novitiate in Kilshane in September each year were immediately assigned to specific studies. Some were assigned to study philosophy in Kimmage for two years, while others were sent to the National University to study philosophy and other subjects in arts, science and commerce. Kimmage students following university courses at UCD generally acquitted themselves very well. Over the years they achieved excellent results, securing a high percentage of scholarships and first places in the different faculties, not only at graduate level, but also at post-graduate level.

Those who pursued secular studies at the university had to complete the two-year course in philosophy at Kimmage at a later time along with late vocations and students who were not sent for degree courses. This mixture of age groups and the disparity between students who were just beginners and others who had university degrees led to confusion for the professors when it came to presenting their subjects and also made it difficult for all students.

6. Irish Press, 3 February 1963, Darina's Gossip Column.

The quality of the home philosophy course seems to have varied considerably from time to time. Students who studied ethics and psychology under Fr Edward Leen spoke of his great depth, clarity and vision. He was an inspirational figure to most of his students. Many students who studied philosophy at UCD would try to find time to attend his lectures in Kimmage as well. Fr Denis Fahey whose presence dominated the philosophy course for many years also influenced many of his students. His great concern was to help students understand the philosophy of St Thomas. The home philosophy course was designed for a former age and relied heavily on one author, the neo-Thomist philosopher Joseph Gredt OSB, who published in two volumes *Elementa Philosophiae Aristotelico-Thomisticae*. This work covered all the branches of philosophy, logic, epistemology, metaphysics, psychology, theodicy and cosmology. This was a poor introduction to philosophy for anyone but especially for beginners. The thought of Aristotle and St Thomas was expounded in great detail in the form of syllogisms, but the interior philosophical processes that gave birth to these thoughts was invisible. Novice philosophers, trying to learn from manuals of this sort, ended up being able to recite various Thomistic theses, but had great difficulty penetrating beyond the words. This was an injustice to St Thomas who would have deplored the idea that something in philosophy was true simply because he had held that opinion. One of Thomas' guiding principles was that no truth can be accepted merely because somebody has stated it, or as he put it: 'I am not interested in what is said, but in whether it is true.'

In all of the subjects dealt with by Gredt there had been huge advances for most of a century. These advances were largely ignored although they were well known to highly intelligent staff members and to students. This, plus the fact that the courses were taught mainly in Latin did little to give students a love for philosophy or for philosophical debate. Most students who had to study the course would claim they got little or nothing from it by way of training in philosophical thinking. For that matter many of the younger professors of that period found the course uninspiring. Most of the professors in the 1950s and 1960s were highly qualified in theological subjects, but only one or perhaps two had a degree in philosophy.

Some professors did indeed make great efforts to upgrade the courses. During the late fifties and early sixties, courses in psychology, ethics and history of philosophy were taught mainly in English and did take into account some of the more modern developments.

After completing the philosophy and university courses, students were usually sent to one of the Spiritan colleges in Ireland or in Trinidad for a few years to do prefecting. During this time of formation they gained what was considered an essential experience in teaching and in the running of schools, as most missionaries would be involved in education either directly or indirectly. During these years of perfecting the student ceased for a year or two to be merely a potential missionary and became an actual worker serving the needs of others. As an apprentice teacher, supervisor, referee of games, and through a host of other chores, he made his first efforts at apostolic work and was exposed to the challenge of maintaining a deep spiritual life in the midst of external activity and constant preoccupation with work.[7] At the end of the prefecting experience they returned to Kimmage to begin their studies in the faculty of theology for four years. Many found this return to Kimmage a very trying experience. Again much depended on the era and who the Director of the House of Theology was. There were certainly those who had shouldered major responsibilities during perfecting, who felt they were being treated as teenagers on their return to Kimmage.

The course of studies in theology was dominated by preparation for what was known as the 'Vicariate Examination', held each year before boards of examiners in Clonliffe College. These oral examinations were usually conducted in Latin and each student had to pass the examination to be allowed to proceed to the next grade of orders. Trial runs at the examinations were held in Kimmage before facing the boards at Clonliffe. During the first two years tonsure and minor orders were conferred, usually in Clonliffe College. First-year students were examined on the duties of the clerical and priestly state. The course fol-

---

7. M. Troy, 'Philosophers of the Diaspora', in *Tomorrow's Labourers*, pp 8-9, 1955

lowed was based on a manual written in the 19th century by Fr
Louis Togni, which led to the course being referred to simply as
'Togni'. During the third year of theology, students were ordained to the sub-diaconate, diaconate and priesthood; those
who were ordained to the priesthood helped with parish ministry in many Dublin parishes on Sundays and Holy Days during their fourth year. Some were also called on to celebrate Mass
in schools and convents on weekday mornings.

Towards the end of their fourth year priests received their
first appointment. The whole period of formation culminated in
a very moving ceremony called Consecration to the Apostolate.
It was very meaningful and moving for those going to overseas
appointments – but a bit of an anti-climax for those who were
appointed to works at home.

CHAPTER EIGHT

'The Emergency'

The new scholasticate had barely begun to function when World War II broke out. In Ireland it was euphemistically referred to as 'The Emergency'. The Irish government, led by Éamon de Valera, had decided that neutrality was the best path to follow in the national interest. This policy was best expressed by the Secretary of the Department of External Affairs, Joseph Walshe: 'Small nations like Ireland do not and cannot assume the role of defenders of just causes except their own.'

From a military point of view Ireland was totally unprepared. The strength of the army was 7,500 and 18,000 upon mobilisation. By 1942 its strength was still only 40,000. It was ill-equipped and there was a serious shortage of weapons, ammunitions and explosives. Anti-aircraft equipment was in short supply.[1]

We are fortunate to have all the journals from both houses of study, which make it possible to follow the effects of the war on Kimmage community on a daily basis. Most of what is written here about Kimmage and 'The Emergency', is derived from the journals of both houses of philosophy and theology.

The threat of invasion was not a figment of the imagination, nor could air strikes by the Germans, accidental or intentional, be ruled out. Lectures were given in the city on how to deal with air raids and on the construction of air raid shelters. Fr Gerry Curran, a former journalist, who was ordained in 1939, represented Kimmage community at these special lectures. In his subsequent talks to the community he usually began as follows: 'Let us begin with the simplest emergency – the direct hit'. Precautions were taken immediately. Air raid shelters were built to the rear of the old Manor House and black-out curtains were put on all windows. On 7 September booklets were issued by the Department of Defence entitled 'Defence of the Home During Air Raids'. The 'Blackout' had come into operation three days earlier. Some students, however, did not take it seriously,

---

1. Dermot Keogh, *Twentieth-Century Ireland*, pp 108-09

so a drastic solution was resorted to, and on Monday 11 September, just over a week after the war began, all bulbs were removed from the students' rooms. Such was the state of concern about the blackout that warning was given that candles could 'be forbidden during Mass'. For a time night prayer in the chapel was read by candlelight. It was two months later before bulbs were returned again to student rooms.

Neutrality had obvious benefits. Ireland was spared the full horrors of war and the indiscriminate bombing of cities. Kimmage, however, just barely missed the simplest emergency on 2 January 1941; around 6:15 a.m., students in Kimmage heard and saw two low-flying German planes on their way to drop bombs nearby. An English Spiritan was the only one with the good sense to run for open ground.

Two families were forced out of their homes by two 500lb bombs in Rathdown Park. Two more bombs were dropped on waste ground near Kimmage Cross (KCR). A third bomb fell to the rear of the shops at the KCR, where a number of new houses had been built and where others were in the course of construction. Two houses, numbers 25 and 27, in Lavarna Grove were badly damaged. Most of the force of the explosion went into the air and this accounted for the fact that houses far away received greater damage than those nearest the crater. Windows and roofs of many houses were severely damaged. Several people had narrow escapes. It was on this occasion also that bombs were dropped on South Circular Road. Five months later, on 31 May 1941, German planes again bombed parts of Dublin, leaving 34 dead, 90 injured and 300 homes destroyed.[2] Notwithstanding the bombing and gunfire, students were instructed to remain in their rooms. About two weeks later all were issued with gas masks and received instructions on their use at the Christian Brothers School in Crumlin. The Camillian students who were studying at Kimmage gave lectures on medical care and First Aid demonstrations.

The situation regarding missionary travel was very serious. Some of those who were due to go to the missions after their fourth year of theology were sent to teach in the colleges, while

2. Keogh, *op cit*, p 123, *Irish Times*, 3 January 1941, T. Roche, Notes

others were sent to Kilshane to what was called 'The Forestry Department', to do manual work making drains and preparing the ground for the planting of trees. Towards the end of 1943 some were able to get to West and East Africa in convoys.

The outbreak of the war thus brought an upheaval of normal life in Kimmage. Severe rationing came into operation over the next few years. The purchase of paraffin (kerosene), tea, butter, sugar, coal, gas etc, was controlled by coupons which were issued in what were known as ration books. Soon there was a thriving black market economy, but even that could not alleviate the shortages. A wide variety of substitutes began to appear on the tables: barley coffee, carrot tea, carrigeen moss, black puddings and fried bread. Scarcity of fuel caused acute problems for heating. When supplies of coal began to run out a substance called coke was used. This was the residue of coal after gas had been extracted. It was often mixed with slack or coal dross which had been dampened and it gave off good heat. Turf was also used and for some years students cut and saved turf on the Dublin Mountains. The journals show that the students were quite enterprising in locating trees and chopping them up for fuel and they made good use of the air raid shelter for storing the fuel. Scarcity of fuel caused problems for Spiritans working on the Burse and for those showing promotional films throughout the country. Trains were running on turf and logs. Balloons and gas generators were fixed on the few surviving motor cars. In May 1941, the government announced that the consumption of electricity was to be reduced by 25%. On 17 November 1941, Kimmage students were ordered to forfeit their 40-watt bulbs for 15-watt bulbs, to comply with the government demand for a reduction in the consumption of electricity. Twenty years after the war had ended students were still being supplied with 15-watt bulbs, unaware that it had been a measure for an emergency that had long passed.

The full privations of the war only began to take effect late in 1941 and during 1942. At the beginning of September 1941, the newly ordained priests had to forfeit their egg for breakfast and tea on account of the rationing. In March 1942, bread was rationed. None was allowed at dinner and only a limited amount at tea. In May sugar bowls were removed from the tables and henceforth sugar was put in the tea in the kitchen. By November, butter rationing had become very severe with only a ½ lb allowed per person per week. The families and friends of students and the Burse subscribers made many sacrifices on behalf of Kimmage by sending clothes coupons to help sales of work. Some families from the country also sent butter, as there was hardly any restriction on the purchase of butter for farmers who supplied milk to the dairy co-operatives. Late spring and early summer 1943 was a difficult time for food throughout the whole country. On 14 May that year there were no potatoes for dinner in Kimmage![3]

One event that is recalled vividly by older Spiritans was the dramatic return of 'refugee' Spiritans from the 'War Zone' in Europe. These were Spiritans who were studying in Louvain and in Switzerland. They arrived in Kimmage on Tuesday 28 May 1940. Seven came from Switzerland and four came from Louvain. Fr Con Liddane, who was on his way home from Nigeria, accompanied them from Paris. Those travelling from Switzerland encountered no great excitement on the way, but those from Louvain had plenty of it.

Although Louvain had been bombed for two days before Pentecost 1940, no damage had been done to the Spiritan buildings. On 11 May, the eve of Pentecost, German soldiers began to advance rapidly on the city. The Superior, Fr Eugene Keller, gave orders for everyone to abandon the house and set out on foot for Brussels. This they did before dinner. Students with sufficient foresight filled their pockets with apples.

In Brussels, Fr Keller bought some loaves of bread which they ate dry. From Brussels they embarked on a refugee train for the south of France. After much wrangling with the Belgian authorities, Fr Keller managed to have the Irish members of his community set down about forty miles from Paris, whence they were permitted to reach the capital under military escort.

The next problem that confronted them was exit visas. They were told it was impossible to procure them in less than a week. They eventually got them, and at two hours notice they boarded

---

3. *Scholastic Journals, passim*; E. Ryan, Notes; T. Roche, Notes; Tim Crowley, Notes

a train for somewhere on the coast of France. At last they found themselves at St Malo and from there they were ferried across to Southampton and on then to London. Again they had trouble getting exit visas, but this time they were fortunate enough to meet the Apostolic Delegate, Mgr Godfrey, who helped them with visa officials. When they arrived in Kimmage they were in an exhausted state but otherwise they were none the worse for their experience and were housed among the philosophy and theology students.[4] The good news story at the end was that Jack O'Hanrahan, Peter Lydon and Paddy Hartnett were ordained in Rockwell in June 1940 by Bishop John Neville CSSp.

Apart from some privations and the occasional bit of drama, life in Kimmage continued much as usual. At Christmas 1939, the Philosophers' Dramatic Society produced T. S. Elliott's play *Murder in the Cathedral*. Fr Mellett gave lectures from time to time on such topics as marriage customs in Nigeria. In general there was little or no disruption to the daily routine. Even the building programme was recommenced when in August 1941 work began on the foundations of the philosophers' study hall, shower complex, workshop and a house for lay staff. At this time most of the old farm buildings were demolished. Towards the end of the war, hardship seems to have been more acute than it was in the first years. In 1945 food prices increased and the quality of bread deteriorated due to the poor quality of wheat produced. To add to the burdens of Kimmage, 52 newly professed members arrived from Kilshane. Those who were students in Kimmage during the last years of the war and as late as 1947 have abiding memories of poor quality food and cold rooms. The summer of 1946 was particularly wet and was followed by a very severe winter in 1947. The cold was particularly bad in the new Sacred Heart wing, a portion of which was occupied by philosophy students in the winter of 1946-47 before the heating system was overhauled and upgraded with some of the furnaces now working on oil instead of coal.

The thirteen-year Provincialate of Dr Dan Murphy came to a rather abrupt end in 1947. He had led the Province and

4. PB, vol 2, no 3, July 1940; Jack O'Hanrahan, 'Flight from Louvain' in *Rockwell Annual*, 1941, pp 41-47.

Kimmage through one of its greatest periods of development. Apart from getting the building scheme at Kimmage up and running after a long stalemate, he encouraged academically gifted students to pursue further studies in Rome, Fribourg and Louvain. This new era was also marked by a remarkable output of high quality publications by members of the congregation. Increased numbers of newly ordained men were sent to the missions. Dr Murphy's personality, views and mannerisms so influenced the student body that outsiders joked that they could recognise Kimmage students the moment they spoke.

During the war years communications with the Mother House in Paris were tenuous and in particular there was no possibility of transferring money. So by the end of the war the Irish Province owed the Motherhouse around £46,000 due in Personal Tax and more in Mass stipends. The General Procurator, Fr Letourneur and his assistant, Fr Maas paid an official visit to Ireland in 1947 to recover this money. It was on this occasion that Fr Murphy made his legendary quip which according to eye-witnesses was not lost on the non-English speaking visitors. 'They can say', he said at a public lunch, 'like William the Conqueror in halting English, I have come for your good, for all your goods.' He was summarily relieved of his duties and posted to Kenya. Two years later, however, he was appointed Procurator of the Congregation to the Holy See.[5]

5. M. Fay, 'Finances' in GTAN, p 319; ISR

CHAPTER NINE

Growth in missionary vocations

The success of Kimmage as a missionary-sending college must surely have vindicated those who resisted the pressure to build the seminary at one or other of the Spiritan secondary schools. Throughout the war and post-war years the numbers responding to the missionary vocation and the members being ordained and sent on the missions increased. Between 1935 and 1953 (inclusive of both years) a total of three hundred and forty six (346) Irish Spiritans were ordained to the priesthood and from 1936 to 1953 (inclusive of both) all of two hundred and eighty three (283) were sent to the missions.

In spite of the deprivation caused by the war and the rise in the cost of living, Kimmage continued to send as many students as possible to UCD. During those years (1935-1953) 319 were awarded BA degrees and 27 the BSc. A total of 78 received the H. Dip. in Ed, 40 were awarded MA degrees and 6 got MSc. degrees. Except for the years of World War II students of theology were sent for studies to Rome (twenty-six) and Fribourg (fifty-one). This rapid rate of growth continued up to the early 1960s as can be seen from the returns for the years 1946-1963. The total number making Apostolic Consecration during that time was 435. Of that number 405 were sent on overseas missions.[1]

At last the second level colleges and juniorates had given ample proof of their worth. They had always provided the majority of candidates. Figures for the years 1950 to 1963 inclusive show that 647 students entered the novitiate in Kilshane. Of that number 393 (61%) came from Spiritan colleges and juniorates; the remaining 254 came from secondary schools run by Christian Brothers, other congregations or diocesan seminaries. Despite severe criticism from within the Congregation and especially from the Generalate, the extensive education base build by the Spiritan pioneers eventually paid dividends and in the long-term was to ensure that the Spiritan Congregation would become Ireland's largest missionary-sending agency.[2]

---

1. BG, 48, p 878.
2. E. Hogan, *The Irish Missionary Movement*, p 78.

A notable feature of the staff in Kimmage during its first 20 years as a house of philosophy and theology was the overall youthfulness of the staff in both houses. As noted elsewhere Fr Bernard J. Kelly was appointed Director of Philosophy in 1939, a few months before his twenty-ninth birthday. His predecessor, Fr Jack Dempsey had been appointed at the age of 30. Fr Pat O'Carroll was also appointed to the Directorship of the House of Theology at a similar age. Nearly all the newly appointed professors to both faculties during those years were men who had just completed their studies in Rome or Fribourg, usually with distinction. Most of them engaged in teaching both philosophy and theology. There were still a few venerable members of the older generation who had guided Kimmage, philosophy at St Mary's (1917-1924) and theology and then philosophy at the Castle in Blackrock and Willow Park. Only one of them Fr Fennelly, survived to see the enormous changes of Vatican II and the huge social and economic changes that affected Ireland. On 5 April 1941, Fr John Kearney, spiritual director and formerly Director of Theologians for 19 years, died. A little over three years later, Fr Edward Leen, who was nearly always mentioned in the same breath as Fr Kearney, died on 10 November 1944. Both of these had a wide influence on many generations of students and through their writing and retreats on other religious and clergy. Fr Denis Fahey, who had been associated with Kimmage as professor since 1912, died on 21 January 1954. Between them, Fr Fennelly, and his deceased friends had written a total of thirty-two books.

At this stage something needs to be said about the programme of formation in Kimmage. Formation began with the novitiate which was a year-long period of relative isolation and initiation into religious life as lived by Spiritan missionaries. There was a very detailed study of the Rules and Constitutions of the Congregation, with special emphasis on the vows of poverty, chastity and obedience. There was also study of the evangelical Counsels which were governed or regulated by the vows. This was accompanied by a spirituality course which was meant to deepen the person's relationship to God and Jesus Christ. The General Customary of the Congregation stated: 'The Novice Masters shall have at heart the initiating of the novices very specifically into the spirituality of Our Venerable Father in order to help them to live in the spirit of the Congregation.'[3] In practice the novitiate regime followed the exercises of St Ignatius of Loyola.

In a nutshell, a good deal of formation was concerned with helping aspirants to live the spirit of the Congregation. They were provided with the condition for a lived experience of a way of life at a very intense level for one year. One might say it was the theory and practice of the religious missionary way of life under very close supervision. It involved total immersion into a system that was highly structured and regulated and animated by an intensive programme in spirituality, again at both a theoretical and practical level. There was spiritual instruction and direction, introduction to the rules and regulations governing religious life and plenty of opportunity through a variety of liturgical and private prayers to absorb and internalise what had been learned in theory. All this of course was well punctuated with times for manual work, games and other forms of recreation with seasonal concerts and outings.

When novices arrived in the House of Philosophy from Kilshane they found the same basic structures in place: prayers, meals, manual work, study, recreation. But life was lived at a different pace. A great deal of adjustment had to be made to fit into a larger community and, what was in many ways a more relaxed regime, but one that, in line with Kimmage's primary aim – formation for the missionary priesthood – was more demanding from the point of view of studies.

There was regular assessment of the suitability of candidates for the missionary way of life. Much of this would seem to have centred on the candidate's ability to: live in community with others; live according to the demands of the three religious vows; observe the rules of the Congregation and the particular rules of the student community; demonstrate a spirit of prayer and a spirit of work; undertake the courses of study prescribed for the priesthood. The student, of course, had to do his own discernment and his own assessment as to whether or not he wanted to choose the way of life set before him. Students were helped in

3. General Customary of the Congregation, No 171

their discernment by their confessor and spiritual director – usually the same person. After mature reflection many fine and able persons decided the way of life was not for them.

A type of 'ongoing assessment' took place in both houses each year. In the house of philosophy all were given a list of those whose three years of vows were expiring so that they could write up any reason why they thought a particular student should not be promoted to perpetual vows or even to a further three years of temporary vows. This was a confidential exercise, but the document had to be signed by the person filling it. This was looked on, by some students at least, as a highly controversial exercise. A similar system was employed in the house of theology not merely for assessment for vows but also for promotion to the various orders right up to priesthood. While it might viewed as peer assessment, this was not the case in reality given that at all times there was a quite a disparity in age between students from the different years. It can also be seen as part of an odious control system. To be promoted to perpetual vows and to the various orders the student had to write to the Superior General. All applications were vetted by the directors and staff and finally by the Provincial and his Council.

Every second Wednesday during term time there was an exercise in both houses called Chapter. This was intended to correct the visible faults of the students and so help in the formation process. Students were obliged to stand up before the assembled community and make a remark about some fault of another student. Typical faults included banging doors, breaking the great silence, wasting time, not taking studies seriously, sleeping during meditation, talking too loudly, poor posture and chewing food noisily. Most of the faults pointed out tended to be trivial, but there were times when remarks went beyond the bounds of Christian charity and students were left with lingering hurts. There were occasions when groups of younger students 'full of fervour' straight from the novitiate, with little experience of the ways of Kimmage, made critical remarks of older men; the reverse also happened. On the alternate Wednesday there were General Observations which tended to be of a practical nature concerned mostly with the general running of the house. In both houses students were responsible for the general maintenance and cleanliness of their house and grounds. Chapter ceased in the 1960s in both houses.

The directors of both houses, philosophy and theology, had a large input into the formation process, so much so that the personality and ability of the Directors was of vital importance. To a great extent it was they who set the tone or spirit of the house. During the war and immediate post-war years, Fr Bernard J. Kelly and Fr Pat O'Carroll gave wise, intelligent and fair leadership.

A new era in the life of Kimmage was ushered in by the appointment of Fr Michael Troy as Director of Philosophers in 1949. He had studied classics at UCD, and acquired a doctorate in theology in Fribourg. Appointed to teach moral theology in the Faculty of Theology in 1948, he was promoted to Director of Philosophy the following year. One of his former students has this to say about him: 'His was an enlightened regime. He was a man who recognised that philosophers were adults and he treated them as such. He gave great encouragement to students to use whatever talents they had and provided the means as well' (Ciarán Shanley, Interview). Not everyone of course would agree with such a favourable assessment of Fr Troy. He had little time for those who didn't get involved in athletics or games of some kind.

There was immense talent within the student community and Michael Troy was adept at promoting and channelling it. He also had immense physical and mental energy. He was forward-looking in his thinking and 'brought a lot of new ideas to the Kimmage student community with the purpose of preparing them for a changing society' (Heeran, op cit). He was keen on modern communications, introducing a printing press and setting up 'Spiritus Press', as well as inviting in professional printers to provide courses for a number of philosophy students each year, who were assigned to it as prefects. These students were taught the skills of printing and publishing. Some students were appointed to follow courses in printing in a Dublin technical school or by correspondence. They sat for the Department of Education examinations, and the City and Guilds Examination, London. A very high quality annual magazine, *Tomorrow's Labourers*, was produced by the students with the guidance of Fr

Troy. For the end of the year students produced the *Philosophers'
Review* which usually appeared on Christmas morning. It was a
kind of *Dublin Opinion* which poked fun at all and sundry; nothing and nobody escaped. A team of cartoonists and humorists
produced cartoons, captions and comment, through which student opinion could be voiced.

A variety of new societies began to spring up under Fr Troy's
inspiration, chief among them being the Film Appreciation
Study Circle (FASC), The Sociological Society and the
Astronomical Society. Although founded by Fr Troy, the
Astronomical Society owed its inspiration to a paper read by a
student from Trinidad, Gerry Farfan, to the Literary and
Musical Society, entitled 'The world around us'. For many years
the Astronomical Society survived under the guidance of enthusiastic amateur astronomers who organised night-time outings to
Dunsink Observatory, as well as holding their meetings on cold
starry nights on the flat roofs. One of these enthusiasts, Eamon
Mansfield, built his own fine specimen of a reflecting telescope.
On Sunday mornings the Sociological Society drew large numbers of students who listened to scholarly papers on current
events in Ireland or on world affairs. One of its aims was to
make practical application of the principles of ethics learned in
lectures. Members of FASC did not merely confine themselves
to critical reviews of the technical and moral aspects of films,
they actually engaged in the scripting and production of a number of short films with the help of Fr Troy and finally ventured
into a number of full-length feature films. The last film they produced was screened in June 1957 as Fr Troy was completing his
time in Kimmage.

Each year the philosophy students did a four-week summer
course. The main subject was Educational Methods. Qualified
external teachers were employed and practical lessons with
pupils were given. An examination took place at the end of the
course. Each evening, as well, highly qualified lecturers gave
lectures to the students on a variety of subjects: art, literature,
sociology, economics, the modern Apostolate and Islam.

Fr Troy was always an avid sportsman and instilled a love of
games and athletics among the students, and here as usual he
led by example, participating in most team games. For many

philosophers, who found the courses of home philosophy of little value, the presence of Fr Troy as role model, guide and source of inspiration was a compensating factor.[5] At the end of the academic year 1956-57, Fr Troy's term of office came to a close. In September 1957 he was appointed Superior and Principal of Neil McNeil High School in Toronto and is considered the school's founding father.

Trinidadian Spiritans
Beginning in the 1920s, students from Spiritan Colleges in Trinidad began to arrive in Ireland for studies. The first to arrive was Kevin Devenish who transferred from St Mary's College, Port of Spain, to the Juniorate in Rockwell. He did his novitiate in Kimmage under the direction of Fr Evans in 1924-25. Having completed his philosophy in Willow Park and having prefected in St Mary's Rathmines, he studied theology in Chevilly in France. During the following decades there was a small but steady flow of Spiritan students from Trinidad. A few did their novitiate in Ireland or France, but most did it at Lac-au-Saummon in Canada.

In 1955 there were 12 or 13 Trinidadian students in the house of philosophy and almost as many more between the house of theology and Rome and Fribourg. Most of these students were highly gifted academically, taking many of the first places in the university in their respective courses. They made an enormous contribution to the life of the community at every level including games, societies and other extra-curricular activities. Contact with these students was the first intercultural experience that the majority of Irish students had.

In the early 1950s students began to arrive from the various Spiritan missions in the English-speaking parts of Africa. The first to come were Antony Nwedo CSSp and Godfrey Okoye, a diocesan student. Both studied at UCD and both of them later became bishops in Nigeria. Small numbers kept coming, usually to pursue studies at UCD but some to complete their studies in philosophy and theology after completing their novitiate in Kilshane.

The philosophy community also received students from the Benedictine Abbey in Glenstal. These came after completing

5. Shanley, Interview, *op cit*

their postulancy and novitiate, in most cases to pursue studies at the university. These too offered another perspective on community living and many of those who came here to study remained in contact with Spiritans for life.

Cracks in the cloister

In 1956 Pope Pius XII promulgated the Apostolic Constitution *Sedes Sapientiae*, a document covering the whole area of formation for religious in clerical and apostolic institutes, with the General Statutes annexed to it on religious, clerical and apostolic training. Concern was being expressed in several quarters as well as in Rome at the increase in the number of professed religious clerics seeking dispensation from vows. In November of that year the Superior General, Fr Francis Griffin, wrote to Fr Tim O'Driscoll, the Irish Provincial, and his Council, requesting a report on the matter as it was also a cause of concern for him. A detailed account was requested concerning the spiritual and disciplinary formation of the prefects while an account was to be given of their spiritual exercises, their direction, regulation for visitors and the arrangements for their supervision. He recommended that every professed scholastic do one year of philosophy at Kimmage after completing the novitiate and before going on to study at the university.

In a preliminary discussion the Council favoured the project of a year's home philosophy immediately after the novitiate, since the members claimed that in recent years the condition of work at the university had become more trying for young religious. 'Secular contacts have been multiplied and greater steadiness than ever is required from our students.' Regarding prefects, it was judged fitting that the superior in each college should see to their regular direction. The choice of men for studies in Rome and Fribourg should be carefully made and those in question should be proposed and considered in Council well in advance. The number being sent for degrees at UCD was also considered and it was agreed that there might need to be some revision of current policy. There was a good case for sending only persons of good ability in fewer numbers and for degrees of a more specialised kind.[6]

6. Pro Co, 20 November 1956.

Already Fr Pearse Moloney, who had been professor of philosophy at Kimmage, (1949-1954) and Professor of Dogma (1954-55) was sent to Rome to train at the Angelicum as a formator under Fr Reginald Garrigou Lagrange OP. It is noteworthy that this was the first time that a member of the Irish Spiritan Province was sent to do such a course. This course owed most of its content to the teaching of St Thomas Aquinas and St John of the Cross. Fr Moloney took up his appointment as Novice Master in Kilshane in September 1956. Also in training as a formator at this time under Fr Lagrange was Fr John Horgan who had been Dean of Studies in Blackrock College and Principal of St Mary's College, Nairobi. This was the beginning of an austere and inflexible regime in the house of philosophy at Kimmage to which he was appointed Director in June 1957.[7] There was a reversal of many of the innovations introduced by Fr Troy. Great unrest among the student body followed and over a period of a few years many very fine men left much to the sorrow of those who remained.

In terms of human and spiritual development many found this period of formation a very negative experience. A negative view of self, of the human body, and of God-given gifts pervaded formation. The world was looked upon with mistrust. For instance the *National Geographic Magazine* was censored by strategically placed 'cover overs'. Students who had, say, completed degree courses at UCD and two years of prefecting had to return for two years of home philosophy and felt they were not treated like adults. Most found this philosophy course a waste of time, made more meaningless by the renewed insistence on Latin by *Sedes Sapientiae* and some years later by *Veterum Sapientiae*. To make matters worse they were not encouraged, and at times were refused permission, to engage in any meaningful pursuit of other interests such as learning languages. Post-graduate courses were stopped; fortunately, these were restored by Fr O'Driscoll and the Provincial Council in 1960.

One of the people who helped to maintain a sense of proportion and balance was the veteran missionary and close friend of Bishop Shanahan, Fr Phil O'Connor. He was a rock of sense as well as being a deeply spiritual man who, as Spiritual Director,

7. PB, No 36, October 1957.

gave encouragement and advice to many who found the regime too much. His friend Fr Jim Mellet summed him up very well when he wrote: 'He passed through life like an angel of peace.'

From 1948 to 1959, Fr Tom Gough, was Director of the house of theology. Prior to that he had been novice master in Kilshane from 1936-1948. During his time as novice master 399 novices made first profession, while during his time as director of the house of theology 340 were ordained to the priesthood. These were the years when the numbers in the novitiate and scholasticate were at their highest. While most of his former students would agree that discipline was strict and the way of life was austere, they also knew that Fr Gough was a man of great kindness and gentleness. He was totally sincere and when he was once reproached by a former student for the type of regime he ran, his comment was: 'That was the system then and I endeavoured to operate it as best I knew'.[8] Fr Gough's comment sums up the formation process. There was a system in place. Students had to fit into it and the director had to operate as best he could according to his own understanding within the confines of the system. Whatever criticisms we may have to make of it in hindsight, we still have to admit that 'the system' produced an army of dedicated missionaries.

Towards the end of Fr Gough's time as director, a year of pastoral theology was added to the course in keeping with the directives of *Sedes Sapientiae*. The course, under the direction of Fr Bernard J. Kelly, began in September 1958 and finished before Christmas. Those who had participated in the course took up their mission appointments in the spring of 1959. From the beginning it was intended to have the course on the overseas missions, but suitable arrangements had not yet been made. After that first experiment it quickly became clear that the overseas missions and not Kimmage were the proper place for the course.[9]

---

8. ISR
9. PB, No 40, November 1960

CHAPTER TEN

Mission House

As the number of missionaries from the Irish Province began to increase so also did the problem of accommodating returned missionaries. In the early days missionaries returning to Ireland on leave were accommodated in the college communities and a small number in Kimmage. Such arrangements were no longer satisfactory to cope with the increased numbers or when missionaries could no longer return to the missions due to old age or illness. Some thought was given to this problem as early as 1924 when discussion took place on the reasons for purchasing Willow Park property; one of the reasons put forward for the purchase was that it could be used for missionaries returning from the missions.

By 1953 the total number on the missions was almost four hundred. This meant that at any given time there was a substantial number of missionaries in Ireland, including those who had returned from overseas, who were entitled to accommodation in a house of the congregation.

In 1947, during the short Provincialate of Fr Michael Finnegan, the Provincial Council gave the problem very serious attention. The councillors were unanimous in their agreement that the issue needed to be addressed urgently. Opinions were divided, however, as to where and how the accommodation could be provided. Three possible solutions were proposed: an independent house at Kimmage; an independent house at Clareville; the provision of additional rooms (12 to 15) in each of the existing communities. Weighty reasons were put forward against a separate house for missionaries at either Kimmage or Clareville. It seems that all favoured the third option which would entail granting a subsidy of £10,000 to each of the existing communities to enable them to construct and furnish the required rooms. Before making any decision it was decided that the superiors of the missions should be consulted for their views. Fr Finnegan carried out the consultation. Of the thirteen extant replies not one favoured either Kimmage or Clareville as possible locations for a mission house. Seven replies were in favour of building additional rooms at the colleges. Two were in favour of converting Willow Park for use as a mission house, while three were in favour of a completely separate residence. Trinidad was against the idea of any kind of mission house.

Fr Finnegan resigned from the office of Provincial in November, 1947, and was replaced on 16 December 1947 by Fr Pat O'Carroll, Superior of Kimmage and Director of the Faculty of Theology. Fr O'Carroll had already communicated his own views on the mission house to Fr Finnegan. He was in favour of procuring another property for the purpose within 10 to 15 miles of Dublin. He felt that the Archbishop of Dublin would accede to the request provided there was no question of taking on a new work. If that failed, he suggested that the Bishop of Kildare and Leighlin should be approached to request permission for a foundation at Enfield where Spiritans already had property. Fr O'Carroll expressed his own concern that suitable accommodation should be provided for those who had worked so hard on the missions.

Almost as soon as he took up office, Fr O'Carroll received a memorandum from Fr. Con McNamara, which left him in no doubt about the necessity, quality and location of the mission house. Fr Finnegan had originally requested the memo. More than any other record of the time it points out the inadequacy and unsuitability of the facilities for returned missionaries, and proposed that a mission house be built with 30 or 40 rooms centrally heated and with all the facilities necessary for people who were retired and sick. The location should be Dublin city or suburbs, within easy reach of doctors or hospitals, university and other amenities. It is only possible to give the gist of the document here, but even by present day standards it is an enlightened document.

Little was done about the mission house for several years. When the Provincial and Council began serious consideration of it again in 1954, Fr O'Carroll was all in favour of having it in Kimmage, having changed his mind as a result of his visit to the missions in West Africa, from where he gathered from the missionaries that they would now like to feel that they were part of the community. An isolated house would tend to make for division between those working at home and those working on the missions. His assistant, Fr Hartnett, agreed with him, but wanted the building separate from the scholasticate. Fr O'Carroll's idea was to extend the old novitiate towards Fanagan's to provide 10 or 15 rooms. At the beginning of April 1955, Fr Tim O'Driscoll, Superior of Kimmage, put forward a more daring and more realistic plan. He placed before the Council the first draft plan of a three-storey block on the Whitehall Road side of the Poddle to be connected by a corridor with the old house. The estimated cost for this building was given as £74,000. All the members of the Council voted in favour of the new building across the Poddle, with some modifications.

The provisional plans which were drawn up by Messrs Jones and Kelly were accepted in principle. The Mother House was not to be informed until further progress was made with the plans. These plans went through several revisions and the final version was not accepted until August 1956. The Council unanimously accepted the final plans for a three-storey building with returns at an estimated cost of £83,000. By this time Fr O'Driscoll had been appointed Provincial Superior, and he continued to press ahead with the task of implementing the decision to build the mission house.

The architects put the building out for tender. Sixteen building firms submitted tenders, ranging from £83,595 to £92,550 and gave as building time periods ranging from 12 to 21 months. The tender of Hugh O'Neill and Co, Builders, Inchicore, was accepted. They were a very reliable firm and the quality of the building bears this out.

Fr Paddy Burke, the Provincial Procurator, negotiated a loan of £20,000 from the National Bank. The loan was made available up to July 1957, after which date it would be reviewed. The reason for this review was that the Irish pound had been devalued, the cost of living had risen, and the receipts from the Burse and Promotions were no longer sufficient to provide for the needs of the houses of formation. Because of the difficulties with the loan, Fr O'Driscoll proposed that the start of the building be postponed until March 1957 and he sent a report on the whole matter to the Superior General, Fr Francis Griffin. This report outlined the reasons for the building, its size, cost, resources to meet the cost, the interest payable and the hope of mission help. It also gave details of the prevailing financial problems in Ireland which explained the conditions laid down by the bank concerning the loan which had been sought.

The Mother House approved the project for the Mission House in Kimmage. The contractor agreed to start in March 1957, and to build at the rate of £2,500 per month. At that rate it was possible that between £15,000 and £20,000 would be needed by September 1957, to meet payments. Fr O'Driscoll asked the colleges if they would agree to lend £5,000 each at that time for three or four months at the rate of interest paid by the bank. This would give Kimmage the credit needed to deal with the bank in September. The superiors of the colleges agreed in principle.

To liquidate the debt it was proposed to set aside each year as a sinking fund the annual allocation to the Province from the colleges. The total from the allocations would come to £7,500 per year. As regards the large sum of interest which would come to about £4,000 annually, it was decided to ask the overseas missions to make an annual contribution for ten years to pay the interest. The sums requested from the missions per year were as follows: Onitsha £1,050, Owerri £1,050, Nairobi £550, Freetown and Bo £400, Mombasa £300, Trinidad £225, the Gambia £150, Pugu College £150 and Mauritius £125. It was felt that a yearly interest contribution would be more effective than the payment of just one lump sum towards the building fund. In this way it was hoped to pay off the capital debt which might otherwise become too great a burden on the resources of the province. The response all round was very good.

As the building progressed, various modifications and additions were made which led to an increase in the overall cost. In June 1958, Fr Burke, the Provincial Procurator, told the Council that the final cost would exceed the contract price. The installation of heat and light was to cost £4,000 more than the estimated price given first by the consulting engineer. A more durable type of plastering in line block was selected for the outside at an added cost of £499. In the granite porch the panels and stained-glass windows of Our Lady of Lourdes cost £290. The total in extra costs came to about £4,800. Added to this was the increase in wages at the time. By the time the building was finally completed in September 1959, the gross total cost was about £108,000.

Very Rev. Dr. Daniel Murphy, C.S.Sp., Provincial Superior, Ireland.
1890 - 1988

Past and Present Promotions Staff in 2009
left to right Eileen Browne, Kathleen Downey, Marie Finnerty

Kimmage Development Studies Centre, group photo 2009/2010

Rev. Hugh M. G. Evans, C.S.Sp.,
Master of Novices, Kimmage.
1860 - 1943

Rev. John St. John Kearney, C.S.Sp.,
Director of Scholastics, Blackrock and Kimmage.
1865 - 1941

Very Rev. Francis Griffin, C.S.Sp.
Superior General.
1893 - 1983

Ordination Year 1968

Novices on Kimmage Farm in the 1920s

Fr. Willie Jenkinson

His Lordship Most Rev. Joseph Shanahan, C.S.Sp.,
Vicar Apostolic of Onitsha - Owerri, Nigeria.
1871 - 1943

Sir Frederick Shaw
(only member of Shaw family to live in Kimmage)

Group of Novices with Novice-Master, Daniel W. Walsh 1914

front row l to r , John Kearney, Bishop John T. Murphy, Hugh Evans, Patrick Heeney and students in the 1910s.

John T. Murphy
1916

Brother Oliver Dowling

The Mission House was opened in September 1959, eleven years after Fr Finnegan had initiated the process of consultation to have it erected. Regulations for the Mission House were drawn up by the Provincial Council. These concerned the length of time missionaries on holidays were to spend in the house. There was to be complete separation from the scholasticate, so much so that scholastics were not to render any services to the Mission House or enter it for any reason. The Mission House was to have its own competent staff of laymen and an assistant bursar was to be appointed to supervise the house. Initially the cooking was to be done from the scholasticate kitchen until the house was fully organised. Residents in this new house were to have breakfast at the same time as the rest of the community.

The Mother House also laid down conditions for overseas missionaries on leave in Ireland. Missionaries, home for three months leave, were to spend one month in the Mission House, while those who came home for six months were to spend three months in the Mission House. Missionaries in the Mission House were to spend two hours daily (from 10 a.m. to 12 noon) at study. As regards rising and the other exercises, they were to follow the ordinary regulation of the community. In effect it meant that missionaries were obliged to follow a regime not too unlike that of the scholasticate. At the time the scholasticate regime was looked upon as the ideal of religious life and observance. In reality, however, the scholasticate regime was designed more for a boarding school situation where crowd control was deemed necessary, than for a community of religious. It was a far cry from the recommendations made by Fr Con McNamara in 1948 that the house should have a religious rule which would be adapted in a broadminded, generous spirit, reminiscent of the missionary life, taking into account the needs of missionaries on furlough.

The new house was very well-built; even modern-day architects and engineers comment on the fine quality of the building. It has been a boon to missionaries ever since it was built and today is home to many retired – and grateful – missionaries. Those who insisted on building this new and larger building rather than a series of extensions are to be thanked for their farsightedness.

Over the years modifications have taken place in this building. The dining room was enlarged by Fr Farrell Sheridan during his term as Superior of Kimmage. In 1996-97 all the larger rooms were converted and made *en suite*, while all other rooms were made *en suite* some years later, usually with two smaller rooms being made into one. During 2009 a new reception area was prepared and a new bright community room was built over the dining room extension providing a much needed recreation facility as well as a community meeting room thanks to the efforts of Fr Michael Kilkenny and Fr Jude Lynch.

In February 1981, plans were made to renovate the Old Novitiate which had deteriorated considerably over the years. All the rooms were renovated, which entailed removing all the old fire places and blocking off the chimneys, and re-plastering the walls. False ceilings were put in place; wash-hand basins with hot and cold water were installed; fitted wardrobes were built in and the electric wiring was renewed. Four large bedrooms were created by breaking down the dividing walls and making two rooms into one. The bathrooms and toilets were upgraded and new showers were fitted. Later, it was regretted that the bedrooms were not fitted with showers. In 2010 all the rooms on the top floor were refurbished and made into small apartments with an *en suite* bedroom and a sitting room or office.

Over the years the Mission House became more and more a retirement home with many of the residents needing regular medical care. To cope with this situation a clinic was set up in the Mission House in 1996 with a full-time nurse, Betty Casey, who worked in conjunction with Mary Hurley, the matron of Marian House. This facility developed into a medical centre, not just for the residents of the Mission House but for all members of the Province especially those who came on leave from the missions. Mary Hurley is now matron of the clinic since 2000, assisted by a number nurses and assistants who provide round the clock care.

Shanahan House
As the use of the Mission House evolved, the need arose to provide accommodation for those who came on holidays from the missions as well as for others who were carrying out a variety of ministries within Dublin diocese and in Ireland generally.

Fr Martin Keane, the Provincial, and his Council decided to build two blocks of apartments on the Kimmage property to accommodate them. The rationale behind the apartment blocks was that if they became redundant they could be sold off or rented without further modification. The architect for the building, employed by Noel O'Meara, was Mr Stephen Tierney. Although not complete for another six weeks, the buildings were blessed in August 2000 by Fr Keane assisted by the incoming Provincial, Fr Pat Palmer. This happened just in time as four days after the blessing the first group of 7 confrères moved into Shanahan House B.

For several years, Shanahan House had a number of vacant rooms which were rented out to overseas students who had come for to study at the KDSC. By 2011, however, it had a full complement of Spiritans, many in active retirement, still carrying out part-time ministry in the Dublin area.

CHAPTER ELEVEN

The tidal waves of change

Since the days of Pope Leo XIII (1878-1903), the church had been trying to move away from a siege mentality and trying to catch up with developments in the modern world. In the middle of the 20th century, Pope Pius XII (1939-1958), set out consciously, if cautiously, to guide the church into the new age. Pius died in October 1958. Later that year he was succeeded by Pope John XXIII who, at seventy seven years of age, was chosen because it was felt that he would not rock the boat and who initially was looked upon as a stop-gap in the papacy. Pope John surprised the church and the world, when in January 1959, he unexpectedly announced his plans to convoke a General Council. The Council was John's answer to the church's problem: how could the church survive in a world undergoing social, political, and cultural change of unprecedented magnitude? How could the church 'dialogue' with the newly emerging world?

By 1959 the world and Europe seemed to be entering a new era. In the previous fifty years or so, profound scientific, technological, cultural and social developments had so changed the conditions of life that one felt separated from the previous four hundred years by a wide gap. Even the term 'post-modern' was coined to describe this sense of living in a new historical era.

It was to this world swept by the winds of change that Pope John announced the calling of a Council. None were more astounded than the members of the Roman Curia who lost no time in preparing to secure control of it. Whatever control they did gain in the preparatory commissions was scuttled in the very first session which opened in October 1962, when Pope John – subtly but unmistakably – disassociated himself from the Curia's narrow defensive view of the Council and urged the bishops instead to undertake a great renewal of the church. Eventually the bishops took control of the Commissions and all but one of the seventy draft documents had to be completely re-written. Fortunately for the morale of the Council the document on the liturgy could be immediately debated as it was forward-looking and provided an ideal starting point, since it was the reform of the liturgy that dramatised for the average Catholic the meaning of the Council.[1]

John did not live to the end of the Council, but he had indeed set the tone for it in his opening address, *Gaudet Mater Ecclesia*. For over a century the Popes had viewed the world as nothing but betrayal and ruination, a place of mourning and lamentation. John urged a different spirit. He was an optimist who saw the world as good and felt that the church should adapt itself to the needs of the world. It was time to move forward, hold on to the faith, present it in ways and in a language that would speak to the modern world.

Pope John died in June 1963. His successor, Pope Paul VI, was elected later that same month. As Cardinal Montini and as John's confidant, Paul VI had played an important role in the preparations for the Council and was now committed to continuing the revolution begun by his predecessor. This can be seen from his opening address at the Second Session of the Council (29 September to 4 December 1963), in which he reiterated the Council's goals: renewal of the church, unity of all Christians, and dialogue with the world. In all, the Council held four sessions between 1962 and 1965, the last three under the guidance of Paul VI. At the close of the second session the *Constitution on the Liturgy* and the *Decree on Mass Media* were produced. In all, the Council would produce sixteen documents, which addressed every aspect of the church's life, practice and relationship with the world.

The *Decree on the Church, Lumen Gentium* was the central document of the Council. This document was a major shift away from the ecclesiology of *Mystici Corporis* of Pope Pius XII, moving away from the defensive juridical understanding of the church, which had prevailed for over four centuries, towards the idea of the church as the people of God which embraced clergy and laity. This renewed understanding of the church allowed for a reassessment of the role of the laity within the church.

Another revolutionary document produced by the Council was *Gaudium et Spes*, the *Pastoral Constitution on the Church in the*

---

1. Thomas Bokenkotter, *A Concise History of the Catholic Church* [revised expanded edition], p 356-359

Modern World. Its overall objective was for the church to begin a realistic dialogue with the modern world. One of the most important debates in the Council was on the document on *Divine Revelation* which, in its final draft, reflected progressive theological tendencies in its acceptance of modern biblical and historical research.[2]

There were further documents which would profoundly influence the whole programme of the formation for priests, religious and missionaries. The *Decree on Priestly Formation, Optatam Totius,* while declaring that the seminary was still to be the locus of priestly formation, announced that it needed to be revitalised. While the seminary would remain a place for formation by discipline it would also be a place where students would learn to discipline themselves. A renewal of studies was called for as well as the promotion of pastoral training. Several other documents were to have major influence on the training of religious missionaries, especially the decree on the *Church's Missionary Activity, Ad Gentes,* and the decree on the up-to-date renewal of *Religious Life, Perfectae Caritatis,* not forgetting the very important decree on ecumenism, *Unitatis Redintegratio.*

The Council was followed by an extraordinary output of theological publications, books, magazines, articles in scholarly journals, all trying to convey the richness of the theology that was emanating from the Council documents and from the vast amount of theological research and thinking that had gone into their preparation. In all its history, the church had never seen such a vast interest in the riches of its theological tradition which had been hidden for many centuries.

Not only was the church undergoing a rapid transformation, society everywhere even in Ireland was undergoing profound change, which became more evident as the 1960s progressed. It is against this background that we must now view the next phase of life and formation in Kimmage.

Fr Tom Gough, who had given eleven years of devoted service to Kimmage and the house of theology, completed his term of office in 1959. His successor, Fr Mike Doheny, took over as

---

2. Bokenkotter *op cit,* pp 361-362; Eamon Duffy, *Saints and Sinners, A History of the Popes,* pp 360-61

Director of Theologians in September of that year. Fr Doheny was the first in this role to have overseas missionary experience, having served in Nigeria from 1945-1959. He had also completed with distinction a degree in Canon Law in the Gregorian University. With his directorship another new era of formation began in Kimmage influenced very much by his missionary experience and an awareness that, like Fr Troy many years earlier, he was preparing men for a rapidly changing society. A new regime, more open and relaxed, came into being. One of his earliest innovations was to allow daily newspapers which were available to students on display boards. They were avidly read by the students, especially during the years of the Vatican Council, keeping students up-to-date not merely in sports but also in church and world affairs.

Six years before the opening of Vatican II, the General Statutes attached to *Sedes Sapientiae* had prescribed for all students for the priesthood some form of apostolic or pastoral activity. Fr Doheny acted on this but there wasn't a lot of planning behind it. Initially for many students this took the form of teaching catechism in the local primary schools for a half-hour per week. Fourth Year theologians, already ordained, acted as spiritual directors to Legion of Mary meetings and Patrician groups. As time went on students were encouraged and directed to get involved in organisations such as *Viatores Christi* and the Overseas Club. *Viatores Christi* grew from a group of students at UCD, who were members of the Legion of Mary who had participated in holiday volunteer work. In 1960 *Viatores Christi* had become a lay missionary volunteer organisation which recruited and trained professional people to work in mission countries. Fr Doheny became interested in their work and prospective lay missionaries began to be invited to Kimmage a few times a year. They usually attended High Mass on a Sunday morning and afterwards met and got to know each other and Spiritan missionaries and students. Fourth Year students acted as spiritual directors to the Legion of Mary who had care of the *Viatores*. Fr Doheny became quite involved with the Overseas Club which had grown out of one of the discussions held in Kimmage by the 'Spiritan Discussion Group'. Many of the students came from Spiritan missions in Africa. The Club was under the care of the

Legion of Mary. Once a year the students were invited to spend
a day in Kimmage and were made feel at home by the theologians.[3] These occasions and contacts provided opportunities for
Kimmage students to broaden their horizons and provided
them with experience of other cultures. Kimmage had its own
celebration of Nigerian Independence in October 1960.
Theologians played Nigerian students in a soccer match in ap-
palling weather conditions. The occasion was attended by the
Lord Mayor of Dublin and his wife. In the evening there was
supper for everyone in the dining room.[4]

While Fr Doheny initiated many important changes and projects they were not always matched by sufficient planning or
oversight. His frequent absence from both the community and
his office on other tasks reduced his availability and was a
source of concern to those who wished to seek his advice on personal matters. These same absences also inevitably affected his
performance as a lecturer particularly in the teaching of homiletics.

As Fr Doheny was settling into his task as Director, prepar-
ations were already underway throughout the country and
among the student body in Kimmage for the celebration of the
Patrician Year in 1961, the fifteen hundredth anniversary of the
death of St Patrick. The year opened with solemn celebrations in
Armagh cathedral on St Patrick's Day. A Patrician Congress
was held in Dublin in June and was attended and opened by the
Papal Legate, Cardinal Gregory Peter Agagianian, Prefect of
Propaganda Fide. On the previous day the Cardinal had visited
Kimmage where he received a rapturous welcome from the assembled community, the Superior General, Fr Griffin, joined by
the Provincial team and many Spiritan missionary bishops. In
his reply to the address by John Geary, one of the students, he
stressed the importance of the missions and missionary work.
He acknowledged his acquaintance with the congregation and
with the writings of Fr Edward Leen.[5] There was a very touch-
ing moment during his visit when he met with Paddy Lewis, a
student who had been struck down by polio in 1955 and who

---

3. PB, No 40, November 1960; BG, 48, p 875
4. PB, No 40
5. MA, Dec 1961

was now in a wheelchair. Paddy's disabilities arising from the polio were looked on as an impediment to ordination. The Cardinal assured him that he would procure the required dispensation when the time came and sure enough Paddy was ordained in 1964. Many other visitors came to Kimmage, including Cardinal Giobbi, Bishop Fulton Sheen, Mgr Anthony Nwedo and Mgr Godfrey Okoye who would be ordained Bishop of Port Harcourt in September that year.[6]

There was a great missionary exhibition in the Mansion House with stalls prepared and presented by the many missionary congregations. The students in Kimmage cooperated with the Promotions and Burse team in preparing a very fine stall. Students studying geography at UCD prepared a magnificent relief map of Africa in fibre glass displaying Spiritan missions. Students also took it turn to explain the contents of the exhibition to the great throngs of people who came to see it. The whole event was an immense boost to the morale of the missionary movement in Ireland and to the students in Kimmage.

A further boost to zeal for mission among the students came in 1963 with the opening up of a new missionary venture by a group of six Irish Spiritans in Brazil. This was an entirely new departure for the province and a new approach to mission. The policy was not to take on a mission territory but to allot small groups of priests to different dioceses to work alongside local clergy. There were no large groups of Spiritans such as existed in some of the African missions, so they posed no threat to the local clergy. In a country where there was grinding poverty and widespread abuse of human rights they placed an emphasis on creating and conscientising 'Basic Christian Communities' and encouraging lay involvement in every way possible. The Basic Christian Communities and other associated movements, inspired by Liberation Theology, worked especially for agrarian reform and for the promotion of social justice in many areas of social and economic life. This whole new approach created a great deal of excitement among the students.

Most, perhaps all, of the students in Kimmage took a great interest in the Vatican Council. Not only did they read the newspapers, they read whatever reviews and theological magazines

6. MA, Dec 1961

were available at the time. Books on the liturgical movement had already begun to appear in the library notably *Liturgy and Doctrine: Doctrinal basis of the liturgical movement*, by Charles Davis, and Josef Jungmann's *The Mass of the Roman Rite*. Edward Schillebeeckx's pioneering work *Christ the Sacrament of Encounter with God*, made its appearance in English in 1963 and was a hot favourite with most students. The works of other up and coming theological scholars began to make their way into the community either openly or surreptitiously. This did not go unnoticed and it led one member of staff to complain about it in class. It took some time, of course, for the teaching of the Council to percolate down to the seminaries since the official documents were only published in October 1966.

While the Council was still in progress the staff for the most part made an effort to adapt. More and more the library was being enhanced with new books. To cope with the demand for these new books and to upgrade their knowledge of what was going on many theology students voluntarily set up small study groups. Each person in turn read a book, wrote a summary and distributed carbon copies to the others for reflection and discussion at the next meeting.

During the summer of 1962, just a few months before the first session of the Vatican Council, the Spiritan General Chapter meeting in Paris elected Archbishop Marcel Lefebvre as Superior General. This election was widely welcomed at the time in the Irish the Province. The archbishop was appointed by John XXIII to the Central Preparatory Commission for the Council. By the end of the Council, however, Archbishop Lefebvre had become more and more alienated from the direction the Council had taken, especially in areas such as religious liberty, ecumenism and renewal of the liturgy. Early in his time as superior he moved the Spiritan Generalate to Rome, thus separating it from the Mother House in Paris. Within a year he and General Council were paying serious attention to issue of formation and studies within the Irish Province, but especially at Kimmage.

In October 1963 Fr Charles Connors, General Councillor undertook a visitation of Kimmage scholasticate along with the Brothers' Postulancy. Overall he was favourably impressed with the life, discipline and academic standards of Kimmage. Minor changes in regulations and in material aspects of living conditions were recommended.

When it came to dealing with academic matters he learned that the professors taught in Latin, but almost solely out of obedience and not out of conviction. The staff admitted that students had difficulty comprehending the material they were trying to convey. One professor complained that he expended more effort concentrating on Latin than on theology. Another professor acknowledged that he could do far more by way of theology if he could teach in English. In addition to the papal regulations regarding Latin, the Vicariate Examinations continued to be in Latin.

At this time there were twelve theologians studying abroad. Fr John Chisholm, who was still attached to the staff in Kimmage, was in Fribourg doing a doctorate in theology, while Fr Willie Nugent, who was given only a limited teaching schedule, was preparing to submit his thesis for the same degree in Rome. The Provincial Prefect of Studies was asked to investigate the possibility of having personnel qualified in missiology, catechetics and speech.

Fr Connors also addressed the needs of the theologians' library. Improvement both as to content and arrangement was required. Some initial expenditure would be needed to bring it up-to-date, and the wholly inadequate annual allocation would have to be increased. One could not expect students to make use of the library if it was of inferior quality. Another area that called for improvement was that of speech and public speaking. He noticed with approval that the scholastics had done something of their own in this respect by forming the Verbum Dei Society. In view of the effort that was already being expended and the eagerness with which all were seeking improvement, a more detailed programme (smaller classes, progression of courses, etc.) should be made an immediate objective.

As regards the philosophy course, Fr Connors noted that the 'Pass' course at the university did not cover sufficient matter in ethics and theodicy. He noted too that there was no one in the province with a post-graduate degree in philosophy.

On the material side action needed to be taken to improve conditions in the dining room. Action, however, on that matter was already in hand, as well as on lights in the chapel, and improvement in rooms which should eventually be supplied with running water, though at the time it was not economically feasible.

Since 1953 the postulant brothers had been following a two-year programme at Wainsfort House in Kimmage, commonly known as 'Fanagans'. These candidates had their own facilities and their own programme of formation with a daily schedule similar in many respects to that of the scholastics, with their times for prayer, meals, instruction and work. Experienced lay teachers gave classes in various technical subjects such as carpentry, metal work, mechanics and printing following a course approved for the Dublin City Technical Schools. The Director, Fr Declan Crowley, aided by Brother Vincent, taught Christian Doctrine, English, Maths and Irish.

In ten years the Juniorate had sent 35 candidates to the brothers' novitiate in Ardbraccan. Without the Juniorate, the Province could hardly expect to have any more brothers. Yet the Juniorate was in need of much attention and assistance if it was to survive and be useful. The house in general was in need of urgent renovation. While the postulants had a good playing field, they had no facilities for indoor recreation. In wet weather 21 boys aged 14-17 were confined to one room with nothing to do. Their oratory too was in need of renovation and painting. Overall the picture painted of the Juniorate was unfavourable and insufficient attention was being paid to the brothers as a group.[7]

The report on the Juniorate for the brothers was acted on fairly quickly. Over the years Fr Declan Crowley built two fine workshops. To the rear of the Juniorate building a recreation hall was built and was ready for the winter of 1966 with facilities for several indoor games such as billiards and table tennis. All round there was general improvement in the quality of life of the brothers and a strong community spirit developed among them. Although their numbers were small they succeeded in defeating the theology students in soccer 2-0 in 1967. Not satisfied with this they challenged the philosophers whom they defeated 3-2. It is easy to see why, since they had Brother Ignatius (Iggy) Curry, an accomplished soccer player, training them.

---

7. IPA, *Visitation of Kimmage* by Fr Charles Connors

There was also more emphasis on training the brothers as missionaries and the brothers were promised that they would serve at least one term on the missions. Better technical training was encouraged at a time when the missions were crying out for such personnel. By 1968, however, the fate of the Juniorate was in the balance due to a new government policy on technical training which required a three-year rather a two-year course in technical training.[8]

The issue was discussed by the Provincial Council in the summer and autumn of 1968 and it was decided that after 1969 the Juniorate in Kimmage would close (Pro Co, 30 August 1968.) Henceforth the brother novices would receive the same initial formation as the clerical novices in Kilshane, due to the radical restructuring of the whole programme of formation which had followed from the General Chapter of 1968-1969 and the Irish Provincial Chapter of 1970.[9] The Juniorate in Kimmage was eventually demolished, and henceforth all technical training was organised from Ardbraccan.

A further extraordinary visit, by Fr Gerald FitzGerald in late 1965.[10] Prefect General of Studies, took place in late 1965. His report was issued in March 1966. This drew attention to the great complexity of the Kimmage Manor campus for those responsible for formation of students. Staff were commended for the way in which they carried out their duties in such a complex setting. Along with the Mission House the campus was host to the Provincial staff, Propaganda and Annals, brothers' Juniorate, the faculties of philosophy and theology.

The situation in the house of philosophy was itself complicated by the presence there of three different categories: home philosophers, university philosophers and those who after home philosophy remained on to take a university degree in Arts or Science. The problem with this arrangement was that it left little possibility for making allowances for differences of age, ability and maturity, especially when it came to conferences etc. A variety of solutions to remedy the situation were suggested, but for many reasons were not possible at the time.

8. 'The story of "Fanagans" ' in *Spectrum*, No 2, 1968
9. Provincial Chapter of Ireland, 1970, Chap 3, propositions 10-19
10. GB 49, p 154

Although philosophy students were well-housed there were still a number of deficiencies. There was insufficient hot water for showers, while lighting in general was poor and had a depressing effect; lighting was particularly inadequate in bedrooms which were still supplied with wartime 15-watt bulbs! The continued arrangement of ten students per table in the dining room, in spite of recommendations made by Fr Connors, did not make for good manners or easy conversation. It was felt desirable to have a better equipped common-room with suitable provision for indoor games. Apart from football pitches, facilities for outdoor games such as tennis or basketball were limited.

Fr FitzGerald rated the standard of studies as good, attainment highly satisfactory and the range of ability very wide. As many as possible should follow university courses but with more planning to meet the needs of the Province and missions. The situation with regard to philosophy at the university remained as it had been. University students in general requested that they be allowed to participate more actively in the various university societies bearing on their subjects. Students complained about the lack of availability of books set down for compulsory reading for the various university courses.

Students doing the home philosophy course manifested their acquaintance with the Vatican II *Decree on the Training of Priests*. They requested a more positive and complete treatment of modern philosophies and, a fuller treatment of experimental psychology. The treatment of cosmology was not considered satisfactory and the absence of a qualified scientist on the staff was felt to be a serious lack. There was a strong objection to courses being given in Latin and an appeal for more vernacular explanations. Courses which seemed to be geared to the weakest students lacked stimulation. Most students seemed to suffer philosophy as a necessary evil. Dissatisfaction was expressed with the summer courses which needed to be re-evaluated and upgraded.

There were wide-ranging observations on various regulations and customaries. Observance of the rule in general was good. However, a keener sense of personal responsibility for conscientious observance was to be inculcated.

On the issue of staffing for the house of philosophy, it was remarked that it was scarcely adequate. There was still no fully qualified professor of philosophy. The director took a major subject in which he had no special qualification and which absorbed too much of his time. The rest of the philosophy staff was drawn from the theology faculty. There was real need for personnel qualified in philosophy, sociology, church history, catechetics and liturgy. Too many had STLs only. And it was also felt that it would be preferable if staff members had some pastoral experience after taking their degrees.

Much of what was said in the report on the house of philosophy was equally applicable to the house of theology. It was pointed out that the students in theology were men of mature years, whose ages ranged from 24 to 28, an age when many seminarians were already ordained and in active ministry and whose contemporaries in the lay state had already assumed family responsibilities. In consequence the director's approach to treat them as responsible adults and give them wide scope for the exercise of controlled initiative was correct and justified, and the results proved it.

Theology students were showing a greater interest in the subject than in former times. The course, however, was still dominated by the Vicariate examinations which were elementary, unsatisfactory and still in Latin. It was suggested that some alternative system be negotiated with the authorities of the archdiocese, possibly through the Council of Major Superiors.

A very important recommendation was that missiology, anthropology, pastoral psychology and associate subjects should be included in the curriculum along with a more developed course in sacred eloquence. A pastoral bias should permeate all lectures and stress should be laid on the theological basis of priestly and missionary spirituality.

Attention was once again drawn to the need for a well-stocked library, better facilities for recreational and cultural activities, since common room facilities and equipment were poor. Cultural activities other than theology were encouraged.

While a reasonably good community spirit existed among the students themselves in both philosophy and theology faculties, they were too remote from the staff. Neither were students sufficiently involved in the life and work of the community nor were they sufficiently informed, within the limits of discretion, of the affairs of the congregation which would deepen their attachment to both. In this respect, attention was called to the *Decree on the Renewal of Religious Life*. Staff members were urged to take a more human interest in the students and in their life and problems, in as far as possible in such a large community, and create a true family spirit.[11]

A good deal of space has been devoted to the two reports, that of Fr Connors and that of Fr FitzGerald, as they both try to convey the overall spirit of the two faculties in Kimmage while the situation with the brothers is well covered in Fr Connors' report. Fr FitzGerald came at a time when change in society and in the seminary was becoming more pronounced and when students everywhere were more informed of what was happening worldwide in church and society. A whole new spirit was beginning to emerge and was beginning to manifest itself already at this stage even in Kimmage. Up to this time and for centuries before it Ireland, as well as the rest of Europe, was a tradition-directed and authoritarian society. It was now in the process of radical transformation. It is beyond the scope of the present work to pursue this line of thought further, but it is important to keep this transformation in mind when we deal with developments in Kimmage over the coming years. One of the ironies of this whole process of renewal and upgrading of studies was that it was initiated by Archbishop Lefebvre, who would soon show himself so opposed to many aspects of the renewal being promoted by Vatican II.

The recommendations of Fr FitzGerald's report were taken on board. There was a very serious effort on the part of staff and students to adapt to the newly emerging situations in society and in seminaries worldwide. When Fr Vincent Dinan became Provincial in 1966 he appointed Fr Paddy Walsh, one of the professors of moral theology, as Provincial Prefect of Studies. Fr Walsh used his office to secure relatively generous allocations for the library which was henceforth constantly enhanced with new books.[12] Staff members made very conscious efforts to up-

---

11. IPA. Report of the Visitation by the General Prefect of Studies and Aspirants, March 1966
12. Pro Co, May 1967, September 1967

grade their courses within the limits of the resources available to them. Scripture courses continued to be outstanding in quality. Great efforts were made, for example, in the area of moral theology to shift from older authors to the writings of Bernard Häring and others. On the subject of Canon Law the two professors adapted, focusing increasingly on principles and essentials rather than on minutiae.

Two professors of dogma had completed doctorates in theology or were in the process of doing so while a third did a sabbatical at the Institut Catholique in Paris. There were also a number of visiting experts who came to give single, or a series of, lectures. Particularly novel at the time was the series given by Cyril Hally SSC on anthropology. There was speedy implementation of the *Document on the Liturgy* from the Council and much was done to put its directives into practice. The breviary, recited in common, replaced morning prayer and night prayer from the old manual of prayers. Already in 1965 there were requests that the breviary would be used at midday and at evening prayer. Fr Peadar Garvey, a gifted carpenter, designed and built a large wooden altar for use in the scholasticate chapel to facilitate the celebration of the Eucharist with the priest facing the people. As a small indication of new trends, the design of the pedestal of the altar owes its inspiration to the satellite Sputnik 1, launched by the Russians in 1957. The altar was ready for the changes introduced in 1965 and still serves as the altar in Kimmage parish church.

There was also a shift in thought in preparing new members of staff for the future. On a practical level it began with a new policy of sending students to Rome and elsewhere for academic qualifications in theology after ordination. Apart from the usual STL, students were directed to specialise in areas of theology such as liturgy, catechetics, missiology, ecumenics, moral theology and theology of religion.

Pastoral work continued to be very much part of the programme. It was generally welcomed by the students and carried out faithfully. The overall purpose of the programme seemed to be more on the work experience and exposure to the suffering of others – both very valid – without much attempt to integrate it into the personal formation of the students through guided reflection on it. As these were wholly new skills it would take time for them to develop.

Fr Doheny, who had led the house of theology through this first phase of major change, was coming to the end of his term. He was beginning to lose that initial enthusiasm and was already turning his attention to other fields. Being very much an activist, he probably felt constrained by the whole system, but he had done much to bring it in line with the changes taking place.

Although Fr Doheny realised that much of the system of the formation was outdated, he also acknowledged that it was the old system which produced some of the greatest Spiritan missionaries who rose to new challenges and led new initiatives. For instance, it was men trained under the old system who showed extraordinary dedication and commitment when the calamity of the Biafran War affected Nigeria. (That can also be said for those who lived through the conflicts in Liberia and Sierra Leone.) He hoped that whatever new system was put in place would train men of the same calibre.

Fr Willie Jenkinson, another man with wide missionary experience (in Kenya), was appointed Director of the House of Theology in 1966. He too was very much aware of a rapidly changing society. Willie was noted for his personal interest in each of the students, with whom he was respectful, open and honest. He expected the students in turn to be open and honest with him. In the years following his appointment, there was a real transformation, with the teaching of the theology of Vatican II.

A report on the house of theology from 1967 shows that pastoral aspects of the theology course were being given more emphasis. Anthropology, sociology, missiology had already been introduced to the curriculum as well as a more complete course in liturgy. A wide ranging course on communications was also introduced. Speech training and homiletics were receiving greater attention. Pastoral training was introduced as a two-monthly intensive seminar, one month at the end of third year and one at the end of fourth year. This course was organised by the Major Superiors and was held in conjunction with other societies and had the approval of Rome.

Minor alterations were experimented with in the day-to-day life of the scholasticate. These concerned such details as time for lights out, places and times of silence, places of recreation and the use of television. There was also a movement towards the organisation of the house on the basis of smaller groups on condition that they were not artificially set up and were based on some internal interest.[13]

Like all times of great transition it was a time of fervour, of challenge, of misunderstanding, of trial and error. Students continued to be treated as adults and for the greater part most of them used their new found freedom in good and useful ways. There were a few, however, who seriously abused the trust that was being placed in them.

Fr Jenkinson was appointed Executive Secretary of the Irish Missionary Union in 1970. His successor as Director of Theology, Fr John B. Doyle, had just barely arrived from wartorn Biafra when he was appointed to the post. During his short term of office he was regarded by students as a most inspirational director. He was able to challenge students to take personal responsibility for their lives and for their actions and especially for the commitments they were in the process of making.

Fr Christy O'Brien became Director of the House of Philosophy in succession to Fr John Horgan. During his time the two visitations from the Generalate took place, thereby providing 'a mandate' to update life in the scholasticate. Almost immediately after Fr FitzGerald's report the teaching of philosophy was discontinued in Kimmage. All students followed the degree course in philosophy at UCD, where the non-matriculated students were allowed as auditors. This, however, did not prove satisfactory and in 1969 under the directorship of Fr Tom McDonald the non-matriculated students began attending the philosophy courses at Milltown Institute. All matriculated students continued to attend UCD, for degrees either in Arts or Science.[14] In the spring of 1972 the Provincial Council authorised the staff of the house of philosophy to explore the possibility of forming a faculty of philosophy for the first stage of missionary training in conjunction with the White Fathers and Mill Hill Missionaries. This was acted upon and the course began in

13. IPA, Kimmage Senior Scholasticate: House of Theology 1967
14. See Geoghegan, 'Formation' in *GTAN*, p 254

September 1972 leading to a Diploma in Philosophical Studies, approved by the National Council of Educational Awards (NCEA). Later on students from the Servites, the Salesians, the Camillians and Redemptorists joined the course. All Spiritan students took the first year of this course. The non-matriculated students took the second year as well, while all matriculated students had the opportunity of attending university after the first year of the Diploma Course.[15]

Repercussions of the Biafran war
While all these changes were taking place in Europe and Ireland the mission field that had been the pride of so many Spiritan missionaries, namely Eastern Nigeria, was ravaged by war, famine disease and death. For several years after independence, tension was brewing between the Muslim north and the Christian southeast in Nigeria. The Igbos of the southeast, who had a higher education level than the northerners, had migrated in massive numbers to the north as civil servants and traders. To the northerners this looked like economic exploitation. The signal for protest came as a consequence of a military coup in January 1966 by Igbo officers in which two great northern leaders were assassinated. Some 30,000 Igbos were massacred in retaliation and a massive exodus of one million Igbos to the southeast took place. In May 1967 the Eastern province under the leadership of Colonel Ojukwu seceded from Nigeria, calling itself the Republic of Biafra. The Nigerian government under the leadership of General Yakubu Gowon declared war on Biafra and imposed a land, sea and air blockade with the object of starving the Igbos into submission.

Biafra happened to be the area of Africa where there was the highest concentration of Spiritans, 307 just prior to the war. The conflict was to have a profound effect not just on the Spiritans in Biafra, but on Kimmage and on the whole Irish Province. Although the churches tried to dissociate themselves from the conflict, they nevertheless initiated one of the most heroic relief operations to help the hundreds of thousands dying of starvation and disease. A Spiritan, Fr Tony Byrne, initiated the airlift

---

15. Pro Co, 3 March 1972 and subsequent meetings. See also Geoghegan *op cit*, p 279

of food and medicines from the Portuguese island of São Tomé to Uli airstrip in defiance of the Nigerian blockade. Uli airstrip happened to be a very wide stretch of newly constructed road between Onitsha and Owerri in a parish run by Fr Aengus Finucane. Another initiative with Spiritan connections was Africa Concern founded in March 1968 to ship relief supplies to Biafra. It was founded by Kay and John O'Loughlin Kennedy and Fr Raymond Kennedy and soon involved several other Spiritans, notably Fr Michael Doheny and the Finucane brothers, Aengus and Jack. Kimmage students became involved in the relief effort mainly through helping with fundraising events throughout the city.[16]

As the war progressed all foreigners were ordered to leave Biafra. Individual confrères and small groups who left made for Kimmage, believing that things would eventually return to normal. Since the Provincial administration, at the time led by the ailing Fr Dinan, was totally unprepared for such an emergency, and thinking it was only a temporary phenomenon, confrères were advised to seek temporary pastoral work wherever they could find it. But the real avalanche for both the administration and Kimmage came with the final expulsion of the Spiritans from Biafra in February 1970. Kimmage was unable to cope with the returning numbers, many of whom felt under pressure to find alternatives. Many went to the United States and England and quickly found pastoral work again on a temporary basis. It finally dawned on the Spiritan authorities that the expulsion was permanent for all except a few. This led very quickly to planning for new missions and out of this emerged the Irish Spiritan missions to Zambia, Malawi, Ethiopia, Ghana, Papua New Guinea and Mexico. The new mission groups tended to be much smaller and the old idea of a mission territory assigned to one congregation was well and truly at an end. This led to a broadening of Spiritan mission horizons and by 1977 an entirely new venture was begun in Pakistan. These new mission fields offered new challenges to young Spiritans in Kimmage.

---

16. Denis Kennedy, *Memories of the Biafran War, passim*; Tony Byrne, *Airlift to Biafra*

CHAPTER TWELVE

The tensions of change

Let us now return to 1966. In August of that year Pope Paul VI issued a set of Norms for Implementing the Decree on the up-to-date Renewal of Religious Life. In each institute, in order to put renewal and adaptation into effect, a special General Chapter was to be summoned within two or, at most, three years (No 3). The Extraordinary General Chapter of the Spiritans which met over a period of four months in the summers of 1968-69 brought together some of the best minds in the Congregation. The results of their deliberations were the production of an interim set of guidelines, *Chapter Directives and Decisions* (CDD), which reflected the core teaching of Vatican II on religious, missionary and priestly life. They offered a comprehensive programme for renewal.

The whole Chapter reflected many different points of view and was like a microcosm of the church at large. Understandably, many of the issues that were discussed were still in full evolution. But underlying all the documents was the resolute attachment to the specific objectives of the Congregation as envisioned by its founders – the proclaiming of the good news to those who had not, or only scarcely, heard it; and the commitment to plant the church among them. Secondly there was a deep concern that each confrère would be enabled to realise his missionary vocation. These two points were to be of major importance to students in formation in Kimmage from then on.

Before the second session of the Chapter in the summer of 1969 the Congregation of Religious issued the document *Renovationis Causam*, the purpose of which was the implementation of the decree on the up-to-date *Renewal of Religious Life*. This document made the pertinent point that the renewal required depended largely on the formation of its members. This was reflected in the Chapter documents which gave the whole of training a missionary orientation with a strong emphasis on human and spiritual maturity. The whole period of training was to be based on the specific ends of the congregation. There was to be no spiritual training apart from missionary training with a stress on community as a formative element in formation. The spiritual objective of the training process would be to foster in aspirants a living faith in Christ and lead them to a more personal encounter with Christ. Identification of their whole life with Christ would be the source of their missionary zeal. As alluded to already, human and spiritual maturity were to be the aims of formation for which self-discipline and the virtues necessary for human relationships were required.

The whole process of formation was to take into account the social and cultural milieu of students of the time with their aspirations for freedom, independence and the desire to accept responsibility at the level of their age. These were the youth of a pluralist society affected as never before by the mass media of communication, taught from school not to accept passively, aware of their own individuality and demanding the right to share in decision-making not only in the political sphere, but in every aspect of social life.[1] It must be noted that CDD was dealing with a worldwide context and much of what was said about pluralism was indeed true of Western Europe and the North America, in Ireland pluralism was in its earliest stages. Ireland was still very much a tradition-oriented society, always a few stages behind Europe and America.

When the Provincial Chapter of 1970 met it took on board the directives and decisions of the General Chapter on formation. The Provincial Chapter directed the Provincial Council to set up a permanent training committee to co-ordinate the entire programme of formation and to recommend experiments to be carried out. A directive of far-reaching importance from the Chapter was that the prefecting system during formation be modified to allow a period in a mission district as distinct from in a Spiritan college. Students would also be allowed to study part or all of their theology in one of the mission districts. The recommendation on prefecting came into operation in 1970-71 when some prefects were sent to Sierra Leone, the Gambia and Kenya.

As time went on, prefecting overseas affected the relationship between the houses of study and the colleges. In the begin-

---

1. CDD, Chap VIII, nos 329-351.

ning, while there was still a relatively large number of students and prefects continued to be sent to the colleges, there was no problem. However, as the number of students decreased and students wanted more and more to go overseas for training, the colleges felt that they were being discriminated against and the students were perceived by some as being hostile to the colleges. This increased the suspicion, which had existed for some time among confrères throughout the province, about the policy of formation in Kimmage since students, even after ordination, were less and less willing to accept appointments to the colleges. The colleges complained that they were being deprived of prefects which was not just detrimental to staffing but also to the process of getting vocations from the colleges.

Even before the Chapter of 1970, students in Kimmage were eagerly reading the documents of Vatican II and other post-conciliar documents. They were reading much of the new theology which reflected the teaching of Vatican II and the rapid evolution in theological thinking. The thinking and aspirations of the students in Kimmage were reflected in a variety of student magazines, notably *Spectrum* produced by the house of theology, and *Insight* and *Philazine* produced by the house of philosophy. Decades later, one is still struck by the sheer enthusiasm of the students, their concern for mission and their eagerness to be part of the whole process of formation and education. One must be careful about generalisation, because in fact only a minority would have shown this enthusiasm. Nevertheless, they were no longer passive recipients of a programme handed on to them. At this time they were impatient at the speed at which things were happening and perhaps not always aware of the difficulties involved in devising, organising and implementing new programmes.

Initially, at least, while staff were making immense efforts to upgrade their courses, they had neither the time nor the resources to meet such immediate demands. It was several years after the council before new members of staff were fully trained in the spirit of the theology of Vatican II. Begun after the visitation of Fr FitzGerald in 1966, the policy of sending personnel for higher level qualifications in the various specialised theological and pastoral sciences began to bear fruit around 1968-69 and to show itself in more qualified staff in Kimmage. The appointment of Fr Brian Gogan as Dean of Studies in Kimmage in 1967 gave a great impetus to the development of a whole new curriculum. The situation in Kimmage was further improved by the generosity of neighbouring institutes such as Milltown, Tallaght and Marianella in placing a number of their specialists at the disposal of Kimmage. With this staff available it became possible to allow people to specialise in a given area. This kind of specialisation was necessary to deal with the newly emerging culture of the Western World and to carry on the work of evangelisation with greater sensitivity towards other cultures. The day of the nineteenth-century manual of theology was gone and only the specialist in theology could hope to keep abreast of developments in current thought.

Through dialogue between students and staff with students and staff of other missionary societies, notably St Patrick's Society Kiltegan, a new syllabus was evolved which was directly geared toward preparing for evangelisation. As well as the traditional courses in scripture, dogma and moral theology, there was a coordinated course in the human sciences, psychology, sociology, anthropology, comparative religion, catechetics, homiletics, journalism, pastoral care, etc. From the beginning there was an attempt to view the whole programme in the context of mission.

Methods of teaching also changed, with a greater emphasis being placed on personal work in the form of an essay to be presented at three-week intervals. This obliged students to think things out for themselves. By 1969 the number of qualified teaching staff in Kimmage had reached nineteen, of whom about half were Spiritans and the rest from other institutions, with one lay person teaching speech and drama.[2]

In 1972, there were further developments to boost interest in, and upgrade the study of theology. Maynooth College agreed to grant a charter of affiliation to the Faculty of Theology in Kimmage. In view of this affiliation, the Faculty of Theology at Maynooth agreed to confer the baccalaureat in theology at pass level, or the diploma in theology to Spiritan students who completed their theology course in Kimmage up to and including

2. Brian Gogan, 'Renewing Studies', *Spectrum*, No 19, November 1969

the third year of divinity and who had passed the required examinations.[3] Students with the required qualifications followed the same course in preparation for ordination. Eventually these courses were also attended by Redemptorists, Servites and students from Ethiopia who had come to Kimmage to study theology.

By 1972, however, the number of students studying theology in Kimmage was down to 53. Of these only 43 were Spiritans, 9 were Redemptorists and there was one Salesian in fourth year theology.

As all these things were happening, there was a very considerable change in student lifestyle. Gone were the ranks of collared clerics in black soutanes, to be replaced by long-haired and sometimes bearded and unkempt young men dressed in 'civies'. Many in Spiritan communities in Ireland and on the missions were genuinely worried by rumours and reports of how the house of theology in particular was evolving. Like all rumours and reports these gained in the telling. An image became widespread due indeed to the externals of the lifestyle, the rumours and reports, as well as the portrait the students presented of themselves in *Spectrum*. There were, of course, those who saw the contents of *Spectrum* outside the context of a mode of expression prevalent and normal among third-level students everywhere. Members of the communities in Ireland, and those from the missions, were pleasantly surprised when they visited students in Kimmage to find that what they had heard did not correspond to the reality they found. The real truth of course about this period is that in spite of all the external changes taking place, the vast majority of students were traditional Irish Catholics who had come from traditional Irish homes, many indeed from rural areas. And it may be said that for older confrères, especially those returning from overseas missions, the changes taking place in Ireland were bewildering. In a few short months on holiday during the summer, they could hardly comprehend what was happening, especially the new and unfamiliar approach to many of the things they held sacred.

Another new and alarming phenomenon was the plummet-

3. *Irish Province Newsletter*, May 1972

ing of the number of vocations to religious life and priesthood. Furthermore, the drop-out rate among those who had joined increased rapidly. People had become used to exceptionally large numbers of ordinations every year not realising that what they had experienced was in fact only a temporary phenomenon. The pattern of vocations that emerged from the 1920s to the 1960s was a deviation from the norm. The number of Irish Spiritans being ordained went above ten for the first time in 1935, reaching eighteen. Numbers kept rising fairly steadily and peaked in 1955 with a total of thirty-six ordinations. After that year numbers fluctuated considerably with a slight rise in the early sixties but began decreasing rapidly from 1966 onwards. The annual average number of professed members leaving between 1950 and 1975 was twelve, but in 1969 the number reached the alarming figure of twenty-three. When the Irish Provincial, Fr Vincent Dinan, gave his report on the state of the Irish Province to the second session of the Extraordinary General Chapter in July 1969, it was a good news/bad news story. There was the impressive number of 776 Irish confrères, of whom 606 were on the overseas missions. That left 170 in Ireland, more than half of whom could not return to the missions for one reason or another. The work of the Burse and Propaganda was going well and 90,000 copies of the *Missionary Annals* were being circulated. But the real bad news was that there were only 12 ordinations, the lowest in forty years.[4]

As might be expected there was a great deal of unease about the decline in the numbers entering, but more so about the alarming drop-out rate, which for Spiritans between 1965 and 1970 was 39% between first profession and ordination. (The average dropout rate for seven major missionary seminaries for the same period was 38%. The highest for any one missionary society was 44%. During this same period the average dropout rate for all seminaries and scholasticates of all congregations, including missionary and religious was 44%, while for diocesan seminaries it was 35%).[5] So whatever may have been the cause

---

4. BG, July 1969

5. IPA, Report on Initial Formation to Provincial Chapter 1976, Brian McLaughlin, 32-3

of the malaise, it was affecting all seminaries and scholasticates. Naturally people began to search for reasons for it and for some means to stem the leakage.

At a meeting of the Provincial Advisory Board in 1972 there was a discussion of trends in formation policy. Some were shocked at the change in Kimmage and felt that a statement from those responsible for formation might be useful in helping to clear up misunderstandings about formation at the time. The response of the staff to this suggestion was published in May 1972. It was pointed out that the aim of formation in Kimmage was fundamentally the same as it had ever been. There was, however, a new approach to the method of training in keeping with the norms set out in the documents on priestly training from Vatican II.

The new approach laid great stress on respect for the individual person, on freedom and personal conscience, greater personal responsibility, on authority as service rather than power, on participation in decision-making, on dialogue and co-responsibility, and greater involvement in the world.

A new approach was adapted to implement these directives. While the ordinary exercises of rule were maintained, responsibility for attendance rested with the individual. More personal contact with directors and staff was encouraged, with students sharing in decision-making at all levels. More freedom was allowed in the choice of study courses, in the use of leisure time and the use of money. Personal relationships were encouraged by the creation of smaller groups at table, and in the community rooms. Casual dress was allowed within the community.

Staff were aware that the process of change was uneven, mistakes had been made and freedom was sometimes abused. There were problems too arising from the ageing structure of the buildings, the decreasing number of students and the constant struggle with an inadequate budget. Staff were aware of their own limitations in dealing with a changing situation, but believed they were being faithful to the aims of the congregation and the church.

At the same time there was a growing crisis of trust between the Provincial Council and the formation staff in Kimmage. This was added to by a growing tension between those responsible for formation in Kimmage. A contributory factor was that there were two basic interpretations as to who was responsible for formation. One interpretation was that it should be the combined responsibility of the directors and staff. The other view was that it was the exclusive responsibility of the directors with regard to the students in their charge.

In April 1972, Fr Frank Duffy was appointed Director of the House of Theology to replace the director who had been taken ill.[6] In July 1972, Fr Ronnie Grimshaw was appointed to the House of Philosophy as director without consultation with the staff, who took exception to the manner of his appointment. And so the lack of trust reached breaking point and came to a head in the autumn of 1972. Central to this lack of trust were differing understandings of the renewal required in the training programme of students, and differing perceptions of the practical methods to be employed to implement such renewal. Since ultimate responsibility for formation rested with the Provincial Council and its immediate implementation with the formation staff, such a breakdown was intolerable. Recourse was made to the Generalate which sent Fr Donal O'Sullivan, General Assistant, and Fr Bernard A. Kelly of the Trans Canadian Province, to carry out an investigation of the training programme, to restore good relations, and to make possible a united effort at renewal, especially in the area of formation. The report of the findings was ready by February 1973. There were two sets of recommendations: one sent to the Provincial and Council, the other to the directors and staff of Kimmage. Fr O'Sullivan was sent back to Ireland to explain these to each community.

In its conclusions, the report accepted that the training programme in Kimmage was in harmony with Vatican II and with the General Chapter of 1968-69. Implementation, however, was not managed very well and improvements were needed to strike a proper balance between community and individual freedom. Application of the new method required the acceptance of a necessary restriction of personal freedom, and the exercise of authority, where necessary, by the director, under whose guidance all is done. There was grave need for an integrated programme

6. Pro Co, 14 April 1972

of formation at all levels in the province including the continuing formation of its members in the field. What the report seems
to be saying at this point is that there was a theory on formation
policy, but no one knew how to implement it.

The report recommended that a Rule of Life be drawn up by
each student community under the guidance of the director and
approved by the Provincialate. This Rule would stem from the
deliberations of the community, would be a written document,
firm and binding, capable of revision and subject to the approval of the Provincial Council. All stages of training were to
be community-based with the necessary adaptation for each phase.

As this matter has already been dealt with in detail elsewhere, it is not intended to comment on the entire report (See
Geoghegan, op cit, pp 262-63). But there are a few points in the
report that deserve attention: 'The role of the Kimmage directors
is to call their respective communities to action, to guide and
supervise their work until they can personally approve the
result. They are assisted especially by their staffs, working as a
team. By involving the whole community, the authority of the
directors is not lessened. On the other hand the responsibility of
the directors to the Province finds expression in the submitting
of the Rule of Life to the Provincial Council for approval.' The
visitors did not pretend to have discovered the causes of the isolation of the scholasticate community, but they did recommend
that it must increase its contact with the other communities of
the Province.[7]

The Tallaght Meeting
At this very crucial time in the history of the Province, there was
a change in the Provincial administration when Fr Willie
Jenkinson succeeded Fr Christy O'Brien as Provincial in June
1973. On 30 August six members of the Formation Team wrote
to Fr Jenkinson expressing their deep concern over matters of
policy and methods of training in Kimmage during the previous
year. Fr Jenkinson had a long meeting with them on 13
September and a further meeting with the other members of the
Formation Team a week later. All agreed on having a joint meet-

7. IPA, Report on the Generalate Enquiry into the Programme of
Training in the Irish Province

ing of all the members of the Formation Team, which was arranged for the Dominican Retreat House in Tallaght from Friday 28 to Sunday 30 September.

This was Fr Jenkinson's first meeting with the entire team. In his opening address, he called for a greater sense of community in which there would be both unity and pluriformity and where *Cor Unum et Anima Una* would be a reality.

Some members of the Formation Team felt that they could not in conscience begin the academic year while disunion existed among them. In the ensuing discussions, both directors of the senior scholasticate felt isolated and without the support, necessary information and encouragement from the rest of the staff.

From the beginning there were obvious personality clashes. But as the meeting progressed, it became clear that there were broader issues which came to be presented in practical terms of roles and overlapping of functions. Gradually, the problem began to crystallise as both personal and group-related and touched on such vital theological issues as pluralism, freedom of the human person and authority in the light of CDD. A common thread running through the discussions was the inability to communicate, first at the personal, then the practical and finally at the intellectual level. Added to all this was the claim that students were receiving directives from some members of staff which conflicted with those given by at least one of the directors.[8]

What emerges from the discussions is that, despite all the changes that had taken place in the academic programme, with the putting in place of a totally new curriculum, a similarly new system for a programme of formation had not been put in place. Many changes had taken place but these were all piecemeal within the context of the old system. No new co-ordinated scheme of formation had been put in place to govern training from the juniorates up to the end of formation, taking account of the differing levels in the senior cycles. There was an urgent need for a new system to be put firmly in place which would spell out clearly the roles of directors, deans of studies and each member of the staff in order to avoid overlapping of functions. There was a real and urgent need for a written Rule of Life for

8. IPA, Minutes fromMeeting of Formation Team, 4 October 1973

each house in the scholasticate which would be firm and binding. This Rule of Life would arise from the deliberations of the whole community and would be capable of revision, subject to the approval of the Provincial Council, but this had to be done in the context of renewal taking place throughout the Province. Crucially, the whole programme of the renewal of formation in Kimmage according to the teaching and norms of Vatican II could only take place when the same teaching and norms were embraced with equal enthusiasm by the whole Province, a situation that was far from the case.

This long painful meeting finally reached a decision that all would work together as a united team for the coming academic year, which indicated a change of heart, the final fruit of the Tallaght meeting. All, however, agreed to tender their resignations at the end of the academic year to allow the Provincial and his council sufficient time to appoint a new team for the following year.

A further meeting was arranged for Sunday 7 October at Kimmage to agree on the report of the Tallaght meeting to be presented to the Province. Disagreement was once more in evidence and since time was not available to resolve the matter, a further meeting was proposed for the following Saturday. However, in a letter written on the evening of 7 October, the Directors of Formation in Kimmage and in the juniorates along with the novice master and the vocations' director all tendered their resignations with effect from 13 October, 1973. The meeting called for that day was cancelled. The resignations did not take place since the superiors of the Irish communities intervened and persuaded the directors to withdraw them.

The work of preparing and producing a Rule of Life for the house of theology got under way under the leadership of the director, Fr Frank Duffy, and was completed and published by June 1974. Its overall thrust reflected the directives on formation from CDD and the Provincial Chapter of 1970. Among the principles it was stated clearly that: 'The director has a number of men assigned to assist him in this task of training. Together with him, these form a team. The director is leader of this team'.[9]

_____

9. Rule of Life 1974, No 2.1, CDD 343

With regard to structures it stated: 'The organisation of the House of Theology is determined through consultation between students, staff and director. This consultation is carried out through the theology Standing Committee's monthly meetings and weekly meetings of each year with the director.' The Rule of Life covered the whole range of student life, principles, structures, studies, liturgy, spiritual guidance, summer vacation, apostolic work and finance. There was emphasis on personal responsibility for one's own life, but there was also responsibility to the community and director as well as accountability in matters of finance. As appendices it included the constitution of the theology Standing Committee and that of the Theology Faculty Council.

The emphasis on personal responsibility was further elaborated on by Fr Jack McHugh who took over as director from Fr Duffy in 1974. Fr McHugh accepted the fact that the 'primary agent of formation is the individual himself, acting out of his own freedom and from his own starting-point. Formation must now be based on freedom, individuality and initiative. This requires greater maturity and sense of responsibility on the part of the student ...'.[10]

The last director of the House of Theology in the old scholasticate was Fr Roddy Curran who took up his duties there in the autumn of 1979. The story of the closing of the old scholasticate will be taken up later. For the moment let us look at other developments.

At a meeting in September 1975, attended by the Provincial and the councillor for formation along with the superior of Kimmage, the academic staffs of the faculties of philosophy and theology, the post of rector of Holy Ghost Missionary College was introduced and the terms of the post were agreed. The rector was to be assistant to the superior of Kimmage, with autonomy with regard to what involves the college. He was to relate to the superior in what concerns the Kimmage community as a whole. The aim of the post was to facilitate animation and unity among the Spiritan staff in the college and to help in the

10. Information/Documentation, 18, 1978; quoted in Geoghegan, *op cit*, p 272

co-ordination of various works of the college. Fr Tony Geoghegan was appointed rector for the academic year 1975-76.[11] Overall this was an important development, bringing harmony to all faculties and guaranteeing the autonomy of the faculties of philosophy and theology.

New Ventures – What to do?

As noted already, numbers in Kimmage had fallen dramatically by 1970. Other developments, however, were taking place. In an unusual development, Kimmage played host to a one-year, part-time course for missionary sisters organised by the Irish Missionary Union (IMU). During the first year, which began in the autumn of 1971, thirty sisters took part in the course. Kimmage offered the theologians' study hall for lectures. For their common room, the sisters used the TV room of the Kimmage staff fathers. This course continued for a number of years and was followed by another course for novices in formation.

    Another major project got under way in 1974 with the establishment of the Development Education course. This was partly a course in fourth-year theology and partly a pre-mission orientation course for those newly ordained. In its early years it was part of the theology faculty and part of the formation programme of the Irish Province. Initially, it was under the direction of Fr Liam Carey, a Dublin diocesan priest, assisted by Fr Jerry Creedon CSSp. This was to become the successful seeding ground of today's Kimmage Development Studies Centre (KDSC). It could be said that this was an early recognition by the Spiritans of the profound changes in mission and pastoral ministry that were sweeping through the period since Vatican II. Although the course, in its early years, catered almost exclusively for Spiritans and other religious congregations, by the late 1970s an increasing number of applicants, particularly those working in the rapidly-growing overseas aid sector, were seeking admission to the course. No other course in development studies existed in Ireland at this time.[12]

---

11. *Irish Newsletter*, June 1976

12. Richard Quinn, *History of DSC. The Development Studies Centre 1974-1998*; Paddy Reilly, *Brief History of Kimmage DSC and Holy Ghost College*

The course had two main focal points: individual counselling and community development. The curriculum reflected the nature of the course, ranging from inputs from pastoral theology, missiology and counselling, some inputs from the social science disciplines such as anthropology and still others of a practical nature such as motor mechanics. In addition there were courses in accountancy and organisational management. From 1976 onwards it gradually became more exclusively mission-oriented.

Major changes began to take place in the course with the appointment of Fr Richard Quinn as first full-time director in 1977. Fr Quinn, whose qualifications included a doctorate in economics, was committed to ensuring the viability of the course, and sharpening its focus, and to the ideals of adult education.

In 1978, Fr Quinn took the initiative in inviting the Minister for Foreign Affairs, Michael O'Kennedy, to present the end-of-year diplomas. The Minister was accompanied by Dermot Gallagher, a counsellor at the Department of Foreign Affairs (DFA), who suggested that the director submit a request for funding to the DFA for a grant-in-aid to the socio-economic aspects of the programme and for secretarial assistance to himself. This was in the early stages of the Bilateral Aid Programme and was the beginning of the association between the DFA and the development course.

The laborious process of seeking accreditation was begun immediately by Fr Quinn. In 1980 the course finally received recognition from the NCEA and from 23 November 1981 National Diplomas in Development Studies were conferred for the first time.[13] We shall return to deal with the continued growth of the KDSC at a later time. Meanwhile there were other developments.

Developments in the House of Philosophy
Fr Tom McDonald was appointed Director of the House of Philosophy in 1968. Prior to that, he had worked for some years in Nigeria. He was a very reflective person who thought things out before making statements or decisions. Students remember him as a good listener who was interested in them and respectful of their views.

13. Quinn, *op cit*, Reilly, *op cit*

Fr Ronnie Grimshaw had taken over as Director of the House of Philosophy in July 1972. Under his guidance a new lifestyle began to develop in the house. There was daily celebration of the Eucharist, with morning, evening and night prayer recited communally. Each student was personally responsible for a daily period of private prayer. The usual annual retreat and a day of reflection per month were retained. As an aid to community integration, small groups of six or seven students met once a week for discussion, prayer and recreation, while the director, staff and students formed a community.

It was recognised that good community life and personal prayer were essential to the practice of celibacy and religious life in general. Since friendships were considered important for emotional balance and maturity, they were encouraged both inside and outside the community with males and females. These friendships would arise through university studies, family ties, relationships between students' families, apostolic work programmes and the summer programme.

The summer programme involved small group engagement in various types of apostolic work, general employment or language study. It was carried out in an international setting in co-operation with other students, male and female. It served as a 'reality testing' period and balanced the predominantly academic nature of the rest of the year.

Discernment in seeking God's will within the community was done through a Standing Committee of elected representatives. The director had the final say in these deliberations as well as seeing that the decisions were observed.[14]

In spite of the good things that were happening in the House of Philosophy, there was cause for deep concern. Its numbers had fallen drastically and the cost of running Kimmage was increasing steadily. For the academic year 1974-75 the number studying was thirty eight. When Fr Robert Ellison took over as director in 1976, the number was down to twenty eight. By that time there was serious debate about the future of both houses of Holy Ghost Missionary College, Kimmage.

Adding to the alarming financial situation was the further

14. Geoghegan in *GTAN*, pp 277-79

difficulty that there were three or four separate communities within the same institution sharing common conveniences and facilities such as petrol, lighting, heating and telephone. This kind of situation tended to militate against a personal incentive towards saving or economising. It tended to isolate people from the hard facts of living which many poorer people had to contend with.

At this time all of the philosophers were attending various courses outside of Kimmage – in All Hallows, Trinity College or UCD. This meant that for most of the day most of them were out of the house. There was also a certain amount of involvement in apostolic and social work which was normally done at night. These and other factors contributed to the feeling that it was increasingly difficult to create an atmosphere of real community living within Kimmage campus at the time. It was originally designed to cater for a student body of between two and three hundred. Nevertheless these difficulties did not prevent the scholasticate community from being a centre of caring and sharing and in many respects it was a dynamic community. From the outside it created the image of a decaying establishment.[15]

Meanwhile, four philosophy students went to live in a house in Monkstown for the academic year 1977-78. The idea was that they would have an experience of formation in small community living. Apart from university fees which were paid for by the Province, they were expected to be self-supporting.

During the 1970s and 1980s a number of students lived among the poor in such areas of Dublin as Mountpleasant, Buckingham Street and Fatima Mansions. Fr John O'Brien, both as student and afterwards on the staff, was a leader in this apostolate.

---

15. R. Ellison, 'The Future of Kimmage' in *Mission 77*, no 8, pp 1-4

CHAPTER THIRTEEN

Services

Like every other academic institution, Kimmage wasn't just a community of directors, professors and students. A veritable team of functionaries was necessary to keep the community viable. Kimmage students provided many valuable services to their own communities in the areas of serving at meals, cleaning the house, the upkeep of the church, maintenance of the grounds, library assistants, book binding etc, and a considerable amount of manual labour on the farm. Nevertheless there was need for a permanent group of functionaries who looked after the farm, the kitchen, health care and so on. These were overseen by the bursar who was manager as well as financial controller. For most of its history the majority of these functionaries were Spiritan Brothers and some Sisters from other congregations. Several of the brothers, such as Brother Berchmans Cassley and Brother Benignus Flood, spent most of their lives in Kimmage. Brother Benignus, for instance, came in 1944 and for many years was the human voice and face of Kimmage as receptionist and telephonist. Later in life he was the community chauffeur, in the days when there were only a couple of cars for the whole community. This task made great demands on his time as well as patience, but he was very much the cheerful giver.

Farming and Finances

As already noted there was unprecedented growth in the numbers entering the novitiate in Kimmage from 1924 onwards. This growth continued up to the mid 1950s. Thereafter the numbers began to decline at a rate more dramatic than the rate of increase.

Both the rapid increase and the more rapid decline were to have serious repercussions on Kimmage and on the Province as a whole. The rapid increase in vocations and ordinations from the 1920s to the end of the 1950s was unprecedented not only for the Spiritans but for other religious and missionary societies as well. Unfortunately, for over a period of 30 or 40 years, people had become accustomed to accept this extraordinary occurrence as if it were the norm. There were repercussions which will be dealt with later.

The rapid increase in the number of aspirants at all levels led very simply to increased costs. For Kimmage the consequences were very serious. Funds were always limited and for many years building was a necessity to provide accommodation for an increasing student population. Food, clothing and many other amenities and services were costly. Every possible source of income had to be availed of. From the very beginning Kimmage farm had been looked on as a prime source of support for the community. Even when the purchase of Kimmage was first being considered, Fr Thomas Pembroke, Superior of Rockwell, wrote to Fr John T. Murphy urging him to buy Kimmage, on the grounds that so much land nearby 'is a regular goldmine' and '72 acres of land will contribute very materially to make the place self-supporting' (and) 'give substantial revenue to the work'.[1]

When the Kimmage property was bought by the Spiritans in 1911, the total amount of usable land was just over 69 acres. Most of the land was freehold except for the 22 acres in Perrystown between the Puddle and Whitehall Road which was leased from the Shaw estate until it was purchased outright in 1942.

The building of the new scholasticate and the provision of a playing field and other facilities for the theology students used up 11.13 acres of the finest pasture land in Kimmage. The students of philosophy also required playing pitches. This reduced the amount of land available for farming at a very crucial time when numbers in Kimmage had increased enormously due to the presence in 1938 of both faculties. In 1937, Dr Dan Murphy and the council agreed to purchase 28 acres of adjacent land in Templeogue from Mrs Mary Anne Leavy. The Mother House granted approval for this purchase on 11 January 1938, and on the same day the Provincial Council agreed to pay £900 per acre for it.[2] As this new farm in Templeogue was separated from Kimmage lands by Cullen's farm, Fr Jack Dempsey, the bursar at Kimmage negotiated to purchase about one acre from Mr

1. IPA, Kimmage Box 1, File 10 Pembroke to Murphy, 25 March 1911
2. Pro Co, 11 January 1938

Peter Cullen to provide a right of way about 100 yards long to the new farm. Sixteen years later, in February, 1956, Fr Tim O'Driscoll purchased a further 2a. 2r. from Cullens at a cost of £1,061.

Even with the new farm in Templeogue, the amount of land was not sufficient for the needs of the scholasticate especially with the outbreak of war in September 1939. The two hundred-acre farm of Killeenmore at Kill, Co Kildare was bought in January 1940 with all its stock and implements at a total cost of £7,500 with a view to supplying the food needs of the Kimmage community.[3] The legendary Fr Jim White, until then Superior of Kilshane, was appointed to run the farm which he did from 1940 to 1947. During that time the farm performed the vital function of supplying all the important victuals to Kimmage. Teams of scholastics were pressed into service under Fr White's direction during the holiday periods and Fr White believed in availing of their services to the full. He did not spare himself either, but those not inured to such a regime found the going tough though, as years passed, it was his hilarious anecdotes, his personal repertoire of expressions, his mode of speech and colourful Sunday homilies that most often came to mind. At times home philosophy students were being called on to work in the farm in rotation during term-time with consequent disruption of classes. The professors of the House of Philosophy made their displeasure known to the Provincial and Fr Fahey added a hand-written note warning against any displacing of local labour by the scholastics. The farm was sold in 1947 as a more suitable one at Metcalf House in Enfield, Co Meath had been bought instead.[4] Fr Colman McMahon took over the management of this farm until it was sold in 1962 at a profit. During those years Fr McMahon also availed of the assistance of groups of students to help at farm work during holidays.

Towards the end of the 1940s there was a fairly high demand for building land in the vicinity of Kimmage. In 1949, Mr William Fanagan, whose house and lands adjoined Kimmage, thought of selling his whole property. Fr Patrick O'Carroll and

3. Pro Co, 20 Jan 1940
4. Pro Co, 13 Feb 1946

the council decided to buy it should it come on the market. Late in 1951 Mr Fanagan made a final decision to sell and duly informed the Spiritans from whom he requested an immediate reply as to their intention to make an offer for all or part of the property. Archbishop John Charles McQuaid expressed his willingness to permit purchase of the house and a strip of land sufficient to ensure privacy, but he was not in favour of the Spiritans purchasing the entire lot for sale. He felt that the resale of any portion of it, which was inevitable, at a later date would make a bad impression on the public, especially at a time when religious communities were being pressed to surrender land for building purposes. Finally in February 1953 Fr O'Driscoll bought Fanagan's house, known as 'Wainsfort House', and 8 acres of land, just enough to ensure privacy.[5] The Fanagan property was henceforth used as the postulancy for the aspirant brothers.

There was no direct access from Kimmage farmyard to the Fanagan property except by going out towards Whitehall Road and then crossing over the front avenue and entering Fanagan's across the Poddle, somewhere to the rear of the Old Novitiate. To provide more direct access Fr O'Driscoll sought to buy a strip of land from Mrs Margaret Doherty of Kimmage Grove who had approximately 50 acres of land to the south of Kimmage property. It shared a common boundary with the theology students' playing pitch and formed the southern boundary of the old entrance as far as Fortfield Road. Her land shared a boundary with the piece of land Spiritans had purchased from Mr Peter Cullen and stretched from near the cemetery to the proposed new Wainsfort Road, thus giving Spiritans access to it should they ever need it. But more importantly it allowed access across the old entrance on to Fanagan's property. Mrs Doherty asked for £1,000 per acre which was the price Mr Hanna paid to Fanagans for land for development. Fr O'Driscoll pointed out that this piece of land would not be of any value to a developer, but Mrs Doherty did not yield.[6] The portion of land amounted to just under 5.3 acres, but by the time the purchase was completed

---

5. IPA Kimmage, Box 1, file 10, Correspondence on purchase of Fanagans
6. Pro Co, 2 April 1954

in July 1954, the actual area was increased to 5.45 acres for which the Spiritans paid £5,228. Messrs Wates Building and Engineering Contractors bought the rest of Mrs Doherty's land in 1955.

About 12 acres of land were purchased from Mr Joseph Kennedy of Templeogue in 1962, at a total cost of £4,250 at a noticeably cheaper rate than that paid for Mrs Doherty's land, since it was still considered farmland.

The purpose of all these land purchases was to provide for the upkeep of an ever-growing student population. At the time of the acquisition of Kimmage in 1911 farm prices were rising and were to remain good up to the end of the First World War when they began to drop.

As already noted, Kimmage farm was looked on as a prime source of support for the community from the beginning. The new superior and bursar, Fr John Stafford, had overall responsibility for the farm. He was assisted by Brother Gerald Heffernan, who had been recalled from Castlehead to manage the farm and kitchen garden. Two years later Rockwell College asked for the services of Brother Gerald in running the college farm. He was replaced in Kimmage by Brother Epiphanius O'Leary who took charge of the farm from 1913 to 1917 when he transferred to the new senior scholasticate located at St Mary's. After Brother Epiphanius came Brother Aidan Cahill, who had joined the Congregation at the age of 30 and who had a lot of experience in farming. His term as farm manager was also short-lived as he was transferred to Rockwell in 1920. For a short time also Brother Mary Joseph Winters looked after the farm. Much was expected of him, but he soon requested to be sent to the overseas missions and he was sent to Trinidad.[7]

To Brother Berchmans goes the honour of having been the longest serving manager of Kimmage farm. He entered the brothers' novitiate in Kimmage and would spend the rest of his life there. He took over the farm after Brother Winters and for the next forty years, farming along traditional lines, he performed his function efficiently, conscientiously and competently. He was a good friend to generations of students whose work he

---

7. ISR

directed on the farm. He was also a most reliable source of news on GAA games at a time when radio and newspapers were taboo for students.

From 1954 to 1957 Fr John Hughes was farm bursar in a new departure of separating the jobs of house bursar and farm bursar. Fr Hughes was a young man with new ideas and a good knowledge of how modern farming was developing. A lot of study, thought and planning went into the management of the farm which was developed along the most modern lines, and Fr Hughes succeeded in raising a top class herd of Friesian dairy cows, which enabled the whole Kimmage community to have sufficient milk for all meals winter and summer, over 50 gallons per day, while at the same time supplying 40 gallons of milk per day to Dublin Dairies. Prior to that, the Kimmage Community had to buy 40 gallons of milk per day. Now there was a surplus which Dublin Dairies would not take and this surplus was used by Brother Oliver in the kitchen to produce butter. This resulted in a surplus of skim milk which was offered to the students who, however, did not show their appreciation for what was considered a generous offer. In fact they felt affronted by being offered skim milk, which was referred to in one famous ditty at a Christmas concert as 'Esso Blue'.

In 1957, Fr Hughes took on the additional role of house bursar when Fr John Aherne was transferred to St Mary's. This was the great era of Kimmage farm. The Kimmage herd of cattle became the best small herd of pedigree cattle in the country, so much so that there was a constant stream of visitors to the farm by farmers who wished to upgrade their own herds. Kimmage herd had up to 30 pedigree milking cows. All the bull calves were kept and sold as bulls on passing inspection. Cattle were frequently put on show at the RDS, and the records show that cattle were never shown without winning a prize.

The farm paid its way and it supplied almost all the meat, eggs and vegetables needed by the large community which, counting all categories, numbered exactly 300 in 1959. The average amount of beef supplied to the kitchen each month was 2,600 lbs, while lamb quantities varied between 500 and 900 lbs. In the farm yard the Revd Philip Lynch was responsible for a slaughter house where he slaughtered and butchered the animals and prepared the carcasses for the kitchen. His work was recognised as being very professional. In later years Brother Peter Mullen took over some of this work.

Between 6,000 and 7,200 eggs were supplied each month to the kitchen. The eggs came from 600 hens kept in two different types of environment, deep litter and cages. The latter were referred to irreverently by students as 'Carmelites'. About 100 pigs were kept and fed on offal and the residue of grain and hops from the Guinness brewery. Fresh vegetables were always available. Fr Hughes did a study of the vegetable market in Dublin and was able to send a constant supply of the kind of fresh vegetables which were in demand at any given time. Wheat and potatoes were also grown, and it was in the planting and especially in the harvesting of these crops that the help of the students was called upon. One year, Kimmage received the prize for the best wheat in the country from Dardis and Dunnes, Seed Merchants. In all this work Fr Hughes had the backing of Fr Tim O'Driscoll who had a very good head for finances and economics.

While Fr Hughes was responsible for the management and finances of the farm, it was Brother Gus O'Keeffe who was responsible for the day-to-day running of the farm, a task which he carried out with energy and ability. Fr Hughes was sent to Kenya in 1964 and from then until 1969 the brunt of the work of managing the farm fell to Brother Gus. Several bursars were appointed during this period, most of whom had little expertise in the running of a modernised farm. At the same time Kimmage farm was gradually surrounded on all sides by new housing estates, such was the expansion of suburban Dublin. These and other factors made farming less viable. Brother Gus asked for a transfer in 1969 and, after a course in Antigonish, he went to Ethiopia in 1971 where he would subsequently play a key role in famine relief. The financial report given to the Provincial Council in March, 1971, showed that the farm had apparently been a liability for the previous two years. Expert advice was to be taken and a report made after a professional survey had been done and its recommendations considered. A few months later in May, 1971, an offer was made to buy Kimmage land.[8]

Already Kimmage farm had been diminished by the building

8. John Hughes, Interview

of Templeogue College which had been requested of Fr O'Driscoll by Archbishop McQuaid in the autumn of 1962. By December 1964, the plans for the new college were ready for inspection. Four-and-a-half acres of Kimmage land were allocated for the building site. Subsequently another 11 acres, approximately, were allocated for playing fields, all of which were re-organised by agreement with the sale of Kimmage lands in July 1995.

In October, 1971, the Provincial and his council decided to engage the firm of Mr Donal Ó Buachalla as sole agent in respect of the sale of land. By January of the following year, the holding of land had been surveyed and by June the council had decided that all lands south of the new Templeville Road would be offered for sale. In February, 1972 the Provincial, Fr Christy O'Brien, notified Archbishop McQuaid of the decision to dispose of farmland attached to Kimmage, retaining only what was necessary for the senior scholasticate and Templeogue College.

The Spiritans were approached by the archbishop in October through Fr Paul Boland to see if it was possible that they might arrange to provide, free of charge or at a very low cost, 5 acres of land to the St Laurence O'Toole Diocesan Trust for a school site at the new parish of Willington. As the Spiritans did not have land at Willington a transfer of land was eventually arranged with Crampton Housing Ltd. The Spiritans exchanged five acres of land in Templeogue with Cramptons who then gave five acres at the required location to Willington parish. On this land the parish eventually built Bishop Shanahan Primary School. In a similar deal the Columban Fathers, who had property in Templeogue, gave seven acres, of which two acres were for the church site and five acres for the Bishop Galvin Primary School.

Beginning about 1973, St Mary's Rugby Club entered negotiations with the Provincial, Fr Christy O'Brien and then his successor, Fr Willie Jenkinson, to acquire land from the Spiritans in Templeogue. The club eventually bought 11 acres of land just to the south of the new Templeville Road, a site which incidentally had been originally ear-marked for Templeogue College. Again, in 1973, Dublin Co Council acquired 1a. 26½p. of land on the southern boundary of Templeogue College for the new Templeville Road at an agreed purchase price of £5,000. As this transaction was not completed until August, 1980, the cheque received was in the sum of £8,219, the extra money being the interest on the purchase money which had been held on deposit since 1974.

The Leinster Branch of the Badminton Union of Ireland, which had a Badminton Hall off Whitehall Road at the western end of Kimmage farm, approached Fr Watters, the Provincial Procurator, in 1974, to buy half an acre of land between the badminton hall and the Poddle in order to extend their premises. This deal was completed by Fr Denis Foley, in September 1974. There still remained 27.86 acres of land in Templeogue which needed to be sold. In February 1977, sale of these lands had been negotiated and a contract sealed with Connolly Construction Company Ltd, who kept the land for some time and re-sold their contract to Sorohan Brothers. The gross price received by the Spiritans was £658,406, and the net price after commission, fees and other cost came to £616,078.

In 1992, with a sizeable amount of land fronting Whitehall Road along with land between the Poddle and Templeogue College, the Provincial, Fr Brian McLaughlin, and the Provincial Council presented Dublin County Council with a plan seeking overall permission for the development of Kimmage lands. This plan included proposals for the extension of the community cemetery, housing development in the old farmyard and along Whitehall Road and a housing scheme for five Traveller families on the back avenue near the Poddle.

It was at this time too that agreement was reached with Templeogue College to reduce the extent of the playing fields to ten acres. In November 1992, An Bord Pleanála refused planning permission for the corporate plan for developing Kimmage lands. Two reasons were advanced for the refusal: the existing deficiency in the provision of surface water drainage facilities, and the desire to preserve the open character of the lands. After this the Provincial Council, with the help of expert technical advice, reviewed the various options available. A further attempt to get planning permission also failed. Fr Martin Keane took over as Provincial with a new administration in September 1994. This new administration eventually decided to sell 34 acres of the land to Flynn and O'Flaherty Properties Ltd. The transaction was completed in July, 1995. The gross price received was £7.2

million, of which 10% went in the various costs, fees and commission. Included in the 34 acres were the 5.45 acres bought from Mrs Doherty in 1955 at £1,000 per acre. They now fetched over £211,000 per acre. Times had surely changed. The land has now been built on, and Kimmage community, with its various buildings standing on a total site area of 16 acres, is completely surrounded by residential development.

Feeding the Multitudes

When Kimmage was founded there was concern that food should be adequate and well prepared. Through a request made by Fr John Stafford, the Superior, Brother Dismas Zimmermann from Alsace was appointed to Kimmage to take charge of the kitchen and catering. Brother Dismas, who had trained as chef and caterer in Strasbourg, proved himself to be a highly competent chef and manager. Yet, In 1916 he was transferred to Blackrock College and from then until 1925 a succession of brothers took charge of the catering. For the next thirteen years, Brother Finian O'Mahony had charge of the kitchen and catering. Up to 1938 the kitchen was in the basement of the Manor House with a stairs leading up to the dining room, which was immediately to the right of the entrance to the Old Novitiate.

With the opening of the new scholasticate in 1938, Dr Dan Murphy and the council felt it was desirable to have religious sisters take over the running of the kitchen along with the infirmary. Approaches were made to a number of sisters' congregations and eventually the Sisters of St Joseph of Peace accepted to take on the task in February 1940. In December 1948, the Sisters were withdrawn from Kimmage, to be replaced on a temporary basis by the Medical Missionaries of Mary, who were not keen to have anything to do with the kitchen and catering, but did take on the task until someone could be found to take up the job permanently.

In August 1950, Brother Oliver Dowling was appointed to take charge of the kitchen and catering in Kimmage. He began work the following month. For the next eighteen years he managed the kitchen and showed himself to have excellent managerial skills. For a month or so in 1951 he went to the Mother House in Paris to study catering with the French brothers. In his work he was assisted by several lay employees, some of whom had their living quarters on the property. One of Brother Oliver's duties was to recruit and supervise staff and, if necessary, to train them. In this matter the bursar gave him complete freedom, which he used very wisely.

In design and equipment the kitchen was the most up-to-date that could be had at the time. It was spacious, bright and airy, with plenty of storage space and good preparation rooms. There was ample cold-storage for meat, dairy products and other perishable goods. Next to the kitchen was a spacious serving area complete with hot presses. Nearby was the wash-up area with plenty of storage space for cutlery and delph.

Cooking facilities were the best that could be had at the time. There was an anthracite ESSE cooker with three large ovens and a gas cooker with four large ovens. A notable feature of the kitchen was the six large, steam-heated boilers and the potato steamer. The boilers were used to make porridge, cook vegetables, and make soup as well as making tea in bulk. One was a very special boiler which was like a double saucepan, and was used for making milk pudding. Each boiler had a direct supply of water. Other equipment included a machine used to prepare crumbs from left-over bread to make bread pudding. It had been used by Revd Philip Lynch prior to 1950 to make sausages. There was lots of other gadgetry, including the meat slicer and an ingenious little machine for peeling apples.

The dining room was a very simple large rectangular building that lent itself easily to decoration. There were two rows of large tables each of which seated ten students. Each table was covered with a white linen table cloth which was changed and ironed every week. Each student had a linen serviette with a ring to identify the owner. At the end of the dining room furthest from the kitchen was the 'fathers' table' on a raised platform. At this table sat the directors and the scholasticate staff.

On the wall above hung a very large copy of *The Last Supper*, by Leonardo da Vinci. On the wall nearest the kitchen were two murals of Alpine scenes painted by Fr Paddy Coughlan. The walls around the dining room had various smaller copies of paintings of no great artistic merit.

Meals in the dining room were served by the students, who

were allocated their times for serving by a student known as the first refectorian, the equivalent of a head waiter. He had a number of assistants, who had very specific duties before and after all meals for one semester. All communications with the kitchen came through the first refectorian, who was one of the few authorised to enter the kitchen on business. The refectorians were all from the faculty of philosophy, possibly because they were younger and more easily dealt with. Other student functionaries who assisted in the dining room were the bread man, the butter man and the milk man. The bread man was responsible for ordering the bread for the whole house and for distributing the bread for all meals and collecting it after meals and storing it in the bread press. The butter man for sharing out the butter, which was measured to a fraction by a machine which was set to cut the butter into circular 'pats'. Each table received ten 'pats' on a plate, one for each student. At one time, these 'pats' were so thin that they were referred to as 'prints', an allusion to the fact that they looked like prints or marks upon the plates. The butter man's task was not an easy one as he was constantly being pestered by fellow students for 'extras', and he also had to cater for the group who were called 'specials', that is students who needed special treatment, for health reasons when it came to food. The milkman's duties were slightly easier as milk was not as tightly rationed as butter was. His job was to portion out the milk needed for each table and collect what was left over after meals and return it via the kitchen to the cold room. Access to the kitchen on the part of these various functionaries enabled them from time to time to help themselves to 'extras' as they passed by.

The directors and staff were served by two students known as 'the fathers' refectorians'. They also served in the dining room for the members of the community who were not on the staff. This was one of the plum functions in the scholasticate. These refectorians took their meals after the main meal was over and were entitled to the same quality meals as the fathers. On Saturday evenings and on the eve of Holy Days they served the late suppers to young priests who would have to say Mass fasting the following morning.

The quality of the food varied in different eras. Much depended on the finances available. During the 1950s the cost of living rose while the receipts from the Burse and Promotions were no longer sufficient to provide for the needs of the houses of formation. The scholasticate was run on a very tight budget, and bursars were expected to keep strictly within the limits of the budget.

The years following on the Second World War were particularly difficult. Bread continued for a time to be of poor quality as the wheat used was not good and wasn't very well dried. In Kimmage, three gardeners, however, ensured that there was a constant supply of fresh vegetables all year round. The farm also produced sufficient potatoes and supplied beef, lamb, pork, chicken, eggs and milk.

The main meal, usually at one o'clock, was a three-course meal with soup, main course and dessert. It was always quite substantial, and perhaps as good as most people throughout the country had at the time. Milk pudding for dessert featured regularly on the menu, while bread pudding was served about once a week. It looked like plum-pudding, but there the resemblance ended. For some reason it was known as 'brown biddy'. Breakfast was usually fairly frugal, consisting as it did of porridge, bread, butter, marmalade and tea. Some mornings fried bread was served with one sausage and one piece of black pudding. If sausages and black puddings were served for the evening meal, Brother Oliver, to confer a little respectability on them, referred to them as a 'mixed grill', while the students referred to them as 'black and tans'! The fathers had bacon and egg for breakfast, and their two refectorians enjoyed this privilege too. There were always a number of nimble students who were able to snatch left-over bacon and egg and other prize morsels from the fathers' table before it was cleared at the end of a meal.

Other students with a penchant for coffee always managed to pinch some from the kitchen which was out of bounds. Certain students were adept at picking locks and having copies of keys made to areas of vital provisions. They were judicious enough, however, to take only an amount that would not arouse suspicion.

Feast day lunches were always excellently produced. The main course would often be roast chicken, which was considered a treat in those days. There were usually two desserts, one hot and one cold. The second dessert was often sherry trifle in which the dregs of the altar wine were used instead of real sherry. Now and then a generous sacristan would contribute a full bottle of wine. Good altar wine, because of its high alcoholic content, was reckoned to be as good as sherry. Coffee was also served after lunch on these occasions.[9]

When the Mission House opened in 1958 all the food for the residents there was cooked in the scholasticate kitchen and sent over in a very good quality electrically heated mobile hot press known as the 'silver bullet'. In 1970, with increasing numbers in the Mission House, it was decided to make use of the kitchen which was already there and make the Mission House a completely separate entity. Brother Killian, who had been trained at the catering school in Rockwell College, took over for a few years until he left in 1973.

In 1968, after eighteen years of devoted service, Brother Oliver gladly left the onerous task of catering manager. For a time he was replaced by Sr Sinéad, a Holy Rosary Sister, who in turn was replaced by Brother Augustine O'Connell for a number of years. Gradually, the task of catering passed to lay staff under the direction of the scholasticate bursar. In the Mission House, Mrs Rose Lynch took over as cook in 1973. At the end of May that year Fr Gerry Gibbons, the bursar, asked Brother Oliver to lend a guiding hand to Mrs Lynch in the kitchen for a week or so. He remained until January 1992. Mrs Lynch remained until she retired in 1985 and she was succeeded by. Siobhán Gibbons, an excellent worker who was very kind to the retired elderly men in the house. Mrs Gibbons retired in 1990 and Brother Oliver managed the kitchen up to January 1992. At the end of June 1992, Fr Peter Newman and Fr Paddy Ryan engaged the services of Campbell Catering to take over the catering for the Mission House and Marian House. At this time the kitchen was refurbished with more up-to-date cooking equipment. A major renewal of the kitchen took place in the summer of 2011.

---

9. Brother Oliver Dowling, *Memoirs of the Manor*, pp 2-19

Sisters in Kimmage

As numbers grew and as the new scholasticate building took shape, the Provincial Council agreed on 11 January 1938 that it was not only useful but necessary for the cleanliness of the scholasticate and the training of young men to have four sisters from Selly Park in Birmingham. Nothing further has been found about this move, but on 21 February 1940, according to the scholastics journal, four sisters of the Congregation of St Joseph of Peace (Nottingham) arrived in Kimmage to take charge of the kitchen and infirmary and they also did sewing and repairing of clothes. The sisters gave great service to the community and were appreciated by the students. Much to their own disappointment and that of the Kimmage community, the sisters were withdrawn from Kimmage in December 1948. Many of the older Spiritans recall the names of the last Sisters of St Joseph of Peace to work here, Sisters Barbara, Eithne, Rita and Concepta. For a short while Sr Mary St John worked in Kimmage as infirmarian.

After the withdrawal of these sisters the Provincial approached the Holy Rosary Sisters to see if they could undertake the work. They accepted the work but could not supply any sisters for a year. In the meantime, Mother Mary Martin agreed to send two Medical Missionary of Mary sisters on a temporary basis, Sr Kathleen Ryan and Sr Gemma Galgani. They undertook medical work only, so the work in the kitchen reverted to members of the community. Likewise, when the Holy Rosary Sisters came in 1951, they undertook to supply sisters for nursing only. The first Holy Rosary Sisters were Sr Raphael Curley and Sr Mary Matthias Saul.

By 1952 Sr Vincent O'Donoghue had arrived and altogether she spent eleven years in Kimmage. She was a highly efficient nurse, who gave excellent and devoted service over the year. For a short time Sr Mary John McNally was infirmarian. Then from 1953 to 1956 Sr Mary Paul McCarron was a companion to Sr Vincent and made a great impression on everyone. Some sisters stayed only for a short time, such as Sr Matthias Saul and Sr Mary Canisius. The sister with the longest record in Kimmage was Sr Imelda Maguire, a lovely gentle woman from Monaghan, who gave sterling service from 1964 to 1977. At this time the workload for the sisters had increased very considerably, since they had responsibility not only for the students, but also for the increasing numbers of sick confrères in the Mission House. This meant there was a great deal of walking between the scholasticate and Mission House. For a short time Sr Imelda was replaced by Sr Rosalie Enright.

Up to 1977 the sisters lived in the convent next to the infirmary in the west wing of the first scholasticate building. After the departure of the Sisters of St Joseph of Peace a recreation area, which was a walled garden with walkways and a greenhouse on the way to the new farmyard, was provided. It provided a quiet and safe haven for the sisters and in later years for students who wanted an illicit cigarette!

Sr Anna Byrne came in 1977 and she was the first to live in the flat provided for the sisters in the Manor building. A first class nurse who had been a sister tutor in one of the hospitals run by the Holy Rosary Sisters, she impressed all who came in contact with her. The last Holy Rosary Sister to serve in Kimmage was Sr Clara Murtagh, a highly competent nurse and administrator. When she was withdrawn in 1987, it marked the end of forty-five years of invaluable service, and the end of an era. The departure of the sisters was a cause of grief to many, but grief mingled with an abundance of happy memories.

CHAPTER FOURTEEN

End or new beginning

Just as the rapid rise in the number of students led to a continuing crisis of accommodation in the 1920s and 1930s, so the very
dramatic decrease in vocations during the late sixties and early
seventies led to a subesquent accommodation crisis of a different kind. There was too much of it. In 1972 there were only 40
students in the House of Theology and 33 in the House of
Philosophy, while there were 26 prefects in the colleges. The
number of philosophy students had decreased to nearly a quar-
ter since 1955. Various piecemeal solutions were tried to make
use of buildings that were rapidly becoming vacant. By 1974 the
Sacred Heart wing of the House of Philosophy had been vacated
and proposals were being sought as to its future use. Four proposals were put forward by the Provincial Council in March,
1974:

1) Use it as a house for retreats and renewal courses.
2) Use it as residence with offices for the entire promotions
staff.
3) Rent it to Dublin Vocational Authorities and thus retain
the essential educational character of Kimmage.
4) Rent it to business firms for storage purposes.

At the Assembly of Ireland in May 1975, it was recommended
that a working party be set up to work out practical plans for the
utilisation of Kimmage resources, in the case of the scholasticate
remaining there and, alternatively, in the case of the scholasticate moving elsewhere. A few months later the Provincial nominated a committee to investigate the matter. That Kimmage
Commission presented its report in April, 1976.[1]

The buildings, so required forty years earlier, had now
become a major liability. Heating and maintenance alone had
become a major financial burden. The most reasonable solution
at the time seemed to be to sell the buildings. Different groups
showed interest in them, but for one reason or another did not
make an offer. Due to zoning restrictions in the area at the time

1. IPA, Report on the future of Kimmage, 1976

it was felt it would be difficult to get planning permission for commercial use of the buildings. Finally, in 1979, The Department of Posts and Telegraphs (later Telecom Éireann) bought all the scholasticate buildings along with five acres of land to the south of the building. The total area of land sold, including the site of the buildings, was 11.13 acres. The deed of conveyance was completed on 24 October 1980.

Already in 1979 the philosophy students had moved to Cumberland House (re-named 'Spiritan House') at 213, North Circular Road, leaving the place with many empty and increasingly dilapidated rooms. Heating a huge building for about twenty-five people was a financial problem. The kitchen facilities were becoming obsolete and were indeed a health hazard. The theology students remained in Kimmage until the summer of 1980, when they moved to Mountjoy Square where they occupied two floors of the Institute of Adult Education for two years.

However, in the midst of these unsatisfactory living conditions, the morale among the staff and students was quite high. There was serious application to spiritual exercises and to studies and a great commitment to pastoral work in the poorer areas of the city. Furthermore, Kimmage had one of the best teams in the inter-seminary football competition and many epic matches, home and away, were played against students of other congregations and seminaries.

The exodus to Mountjoy Square in September 1980 was somewhat disruptive and makeshift, but thanks to the goodwill of staff, students and their director, Fr Roddy Curran, assisted by Fr Tony Geoghegan, a vibrant and happy community developed. Their accommodation consisted of 20 bedrooms, 3 classrooms, an oratory, community room, 2 offices and a dining room. At this time 16 students lived there together with 3 members of staff. A number of students lived in poorer circumstances in nearby Rutland Street, where they worked closely with people of the parish in various projects. Lecturers came from Kimmage, Spiritan House and Marianella Redemptorist Centre for studies, sometimes at great inconvenience because of traffic, lack of parking facilities and the usual weather conditions. In spite of living in stringent conditions there was a good spirit among the students who showed plenty of goodwill.

For recreation they jogged around the square, some played squash in Clonliffe College and weekly football matches took place in the grounds of St Brendan's, Grangegorman.[2]

This was truly a difficult time, a poignant moment for all who had cherished Kimmage with all its warts, but not least for those who had to make such momentous decisions regarding what had been home to many for so many years. Of all the repercussions of declining numbers and a return to what was normal, this was perhaps the greatest in emotional terms. Several, for whom Kimmage had been almost their life's work and who saw it rise to the heights, were to see it decline and lose its former glory. It was particularly painful for Fr Dan Murphy who died there, in Marian House, on 4 April 1988.

The money received from the sale of the scholasticate amounted to £1.13 million, most of which was used to build the new House of Theology and carry out very extensive renovation work on the old novitiate building. Early in 1981, the plans for the new house of theology, drawn up by Mr Brian Brennan, were accepted and put to tender. By February, a contract was drawn up and work began on the building in March 1981. To make way for the new building, Fanagans' house, the brothers' old house, which was the renovated air-raid shelter, the old stores and workshops, as well as the Venerable Libermann corridor were all demolished. The new building consisted of three residences, each with nine bedrooms and a sitting room as well as bathrooms and toilets. There was also a central services and administration building which contained the oratory, dining room, kitchen, library, common room and offices. This new building was ready within a year and the theology students and staff returned to Kimmage on 29 April 1982.[3]

The director of theologians during these difficult years of transition was Fr Roddy Curran. Under his guidance seminary life in all its aspects returned to normal and it was surprising how quickly everybody settled into the new environment. The proximity of the old scholasticate church, which had become a chapel-of-ease of Crumlin parish, allowed students to become

2. Roddy Curran, *Memoirs*
3. IPA, Kimmage, Box 3

involved with the worshipping community there. The Development Studies courses had remained on at Kimmage using some of the large rooms in the Old Manor building, and the presence of their students, most of whom at this time were non-Irish nationals from a variety of countries, was most enriching. With the co-operation of Templeogue College, one of their pitches was made available to the community at suitable times.

Hospitality was a notable feature of this new student community. Relatives and friends were invited to meals and when possible, accommodation was also provided. Confrères on leave from their missions were frequent visitors and were always warmly welcomed. People with varying expertise were invited to give talks adding to the vitality and morale of the community.

In the spirit of Vatican II, the Secretariat for Christian Unity decided in the 1970s to sponsor students, lay and clerical, of the Orthodox, Coptic and Ethiopian Churches, to study in various centres in Western Europe. The purpose was to develop better relationships between these churches and Rome. Dublin was chosen as one of the designated centres and the House of Theology at Kimmage was asked to host a number of students each year. Beginning in 1977 and up to the end of the century, these students had a notable and significant presence in Kimmage. They came from Ethiopia, Egypt, Romania, Greece, Syria and India. They studied in Kimmage, Maynooth, Milltown or in some other suitable and relevant institution. Their presence was beneficial to all, for it created a practical ecumenical awareness and fostered a deeper richness in the theology studied.

In general this programme was very successful. Many returned to their own countries and became leaders within their respective churches. Their experience of western theology and of living in Western Europe helped them to foster ever-improving understanding of and co-operation with the Roman Catholic Church. Kimmage can be proud of its contribution to this practical form of ecumenism.[4]

Fr Seán Kealy, who had previously taught scripture at Kenyatta College in Kenya took over the directorship of the new house of studies in 1984. As well as being director he also lect-

---

4. Curran, *op cit*

ured in scripture in the Kimmage theology faculty, and was much in demand for retreats and lectures throughout the country. During this time there were a considerable number of students from Ethiopia, from the new Spiritan foundations in Africa and from India, who lived in the community and followed various courses in the theology faculty or in the Development Studies Centre.

Fr Pat Palmer, who had followed courses in psychoanalysis and counselling in Rome, and who had been director of philosophers in Spiritan House became director of the house of studies from 1986 to 1990. Later he became novice master of the West African Foundation. His successor in the house of theology was Fr Peter Conaty who had qualified in liturgical theology in Washington and had overseas mission experience in The Gambia. As well as being director he lectured in liturgical theology in the Kimmage Mission Institute (KMI) which was just getting under way. As part of the programme of rationalisation of the houses of formation, the committee set up for this purpose recommended that the students of philosophy take up residence in Kimmage. In September 1995, they returned to Kimmage from Spiritan House, North Circular Road, thus bringing the two faculties together again under one director after a separation of sixteen years. This was also the period when students from the West African foundation were accepted for the course in theology at KMI and they too formed part of the student community at the house of studies.

As noted earlier, Holy Ghost College, Kimmage became affiliated to the Pontifical University at Maynooth which meant that students undertaking studies at Kimmage could be conferred with either a BA in Divinity or the Diploma in Divinity. From then until the end of the late 1980s, the faculty of theology run by the Spiritans and the Redemptorist Congregation continued to receive accreditation for its courses from Maynooth. When the number of students in both congregations began to diminish more rapidly in the late 1980s, the ongoing viability of the faculty was seriously in question. At the invitation of the Irish Missionary Union, a group was formed with representatives from eleven congregations to consider their future educational needs, and they recommended the formation of a new specialist mission theologate. This culminated in the establishment of the Kimmage Mission Institute of theology and cultures with Fr Vincent McNamara SPS as President, Fr Tony Geoghegan CSSp as Dean of Studies and Fr Con Casey CSsR as Registrar. All three, along with a highly competent staff, contributed enormously to the teaching and renewal of theology. It was theology learning at its best, and both staff and students found it a joy to be part of the process. Rather than renew its affiliation with Maynooth, the new institute decided to seek accreditation for its degree course from the NCEA and its submission for a BA in theology and anthropology was approved in 1992. In 1999 a new taught post-graduate MA in Faith and Culture Studies was also approved by the NCEA.

A decision by the Board of KMI to form a strategic alliance with the Milltown Institute of Theology was made in 2003. From September that year all of its programmes were run at the larger institute in Milltown Park. This was exactly seventy years after the theology students moved back from Blackrock to Kimmage in the autumn of 1933, thus marking the end of another era. The KMI became the Department of Mission Theology and Cultures at Milltown, with Fr Paddy Roe CSSp as its first Director. Other Spiritans who transferred to Milltown were Fr Elochukwu Uzukwu, Fr Denis Robinson and Fr Tom Whelan.

After twenty-one years as a missionary in Ethiopia, Fr Martin A. Kelly returned to an utterly changed Kimmage as director of the house of studies in 1996. Students were fewer than twenty, but made up of so many nationalities that often over a dozen countries were represented in the community during any given year. They came from Africa, Asia, the Middle East, Europe – east and west – Australia and Trinidad. During the summer break Orthodox students from all over Eastern Europe and even Ethiopia and India, flocked to Kimmage to study English in Dublin, many of them – monks, priests, nuns, lay men and women – were post-graduate theology students in Rome. Passengers on the 15A bus, which serves the Kimmage area were a step ahead of the rest of Dublin in getting used to the multi-cultural Ireland that was quickly emerging.

Even more cosmopolitan were the KDSC, whose large number of overseas students brought their own enrichment to the life of the campus, and the KMI which, however, represented by eleven or twelve missionary congregations, was more part of the life of the house of studies as most of the Kimmage students and staff studied and taught there. The presence of many other congregations as well as of lay men and women, single and married, was in itself enriching and challenging for the students. For a Kimmage student to be late in handing in an essay was – or should have been – embarrassing when a mother of three had her's in on time. All students and staff took their morning coffee in the students' dining room. Morning coffee with Bobby Farrell's scones is still remembered all over the world not just for the lively theological discussions that took place but also for the friends that were made. Similarly the opening and closing dinners of the year were occasions when acquaintances were made and renewed as well as heart-felt goodbyes tendered.[5] The last Spiritan for the Irish Province was ordained during Fr Kelly's term of office in 2001.

The writing was already writ large on the wall when Fr Edward Flynn took over as director in August 2003. There were eleven Spiritan students in the house of studies, all from African Provinces or foundations who now followed courses in theology at Milltown Park. The numbers continued at approximately this level for several years with one non-professed Irish student in 2006. Most of the African students were eventually ordained and the last to complete his studies in Ireland was Denis Kamangala Mbumba from Congo Kinshasa. The house of studies closed officially on 31 May 2008, bringing to an end almost a century of Spiritan missionary formation in Kimmage.

The Development Studies Centre, however, has remained on at Kimmage under the leadership of Paddy Reilly who has continued to expand and develop the course with huge dedication, imagination and flair. Paddy, who took over from Richard Quinn in 1995, has provided an extraordinarily open and facilitative style of leadership for what is very much a team effort. He and his colleagues show a dedication which goes well beyond the call of duty.

---

5. Martin A Kelly, *Memorial Snaps of the House of Studies*

Since 2004 the centre has begun to offer a two-year programme for the BA in Development Studies as well as an MA in Development Studies and a Post-Graduate Diploma in Development Studies. In the autumn of 2004, a new chapter in the range of activities offered by the KDSC began when Kimmage successfully tendered for a contract to run a training and learning programme for Ireland's development NGO and missionary sector, formerly run by the now defunct Agency for Personal Services Overseas (APSO) and more recently by Irish Aid.

Further developments took place in 2007 and 2008 with the setting up of two other programmes which reflect the determination of the KDSC to reach out to wider groups of development workers and to diversify its activities. These developments were the establishment of the Kimmage East Africa Programme in 2007 and the setting up of Kimmage Open and Distance Education programme (KODE) in 2009. There is ongoing development of the programmes at home and abroad and the forging of new links with such institutes as Sokoine University of Agriculture in Morogoro, Tanzania an area that has witnessed Spiritan activity since the 1860s.

So at least one form of growth inspired by Spiritan missionary idealism continues to emanate from Kimmage as we celebrate this centenary year. The staff of KDSC carry on the work with every bit as much dedication as the Spiritans ever did and keep the the Spiritan ethos alive. We still cannot read the future. But what we do know is that past students of Kimmage's scholasticate, house of studies, mission institute and Development Studies Centre minister and serve in dozens of countries in all continents, enriching the lives of people spiritually, culturally, economically, intellectually, politically and, who knows, even artistically. No one could give an account of the good they are doing. Like everything else, we leave them all in the hands of God. Long may they continue to serve him.

CHAPTER FIFTEEN

Kimmage Parish

Long before the sale of the senior scholasticate, Kimmage chapel had become far too large for the small number of students. Various smaller oratories had been created within the scholasticate buildings, mainly by converting a number of bedrooms to make smaller and more community-oriented places of prayer. At the time of the sale of the scholasticate, the Provincial, Fr Enda Watters, offered the Kimmage Chapel to Archbishop Ryan for public worship. Although the Poddle at that point formed the boundary between Templeogue Parish and Crumlin, thus placing the chapel physically in Templeogue parish, the chapel nevertheless came under the administration of Crumlin parish. The person immediately responsible for its administration, however, was a Spiritan priest, and the Spiritans retained ownership and use of the chapel. Some of the money from the sale of the scholasticate was used to upgrade the heating system in the chapel.

In August 1983, Barney Flynn CSSp was appointed to Crumlin parish. For the next eight years Fr Flynn had almost complete responsibility for the running of Kimmage chapel and all that pertained to public worship there. His ministry was mainly in that area of Crumlin parish which was eventually ceded to Kimmage. Here he built up great rapport with the people and thus prepared for the permanent setting up of a separate parish in Kimmage.

In line with the decisions of the Provincial Chapter of 1988, Archbishop Desmond Connell was requested to authorise the establishment of a new parish at Kimmage to be staffed by Spiritans. Kimmage chapel was to be used as the parish church. The archbishop gave his consent, and the Diocesan Priests' Council also gave their approval. The parish was formally established on Sunday 9 December 1990, when Bishop Eamonn Walsh, auxiliary bishop of Dublin, installed the first parish priest, Fr Des Byrne. Fr Noel Banahan, who had been appointed assistant, was unable to take up duty due to illness. He was replaced on a temporary basis by Fr Paddy Ryan, who continued there until

September 1991, when he was replaced by Fr Christy Burke. Fr Banahan's illness turned out to be terminal and he died on 14 March 1991.

The new parish incorporated a large section of Crumlin parish and a small section of Greenhills parish. As part of the agreement with the diocese, the Provincialate had all the stained glass windows in the chapel re-leaded during 1991. The windows had buckled over the years due to a faulty design in the metal frames, which did not allow for expansion. Some time later all the side altars were removed under the direction of the architect, Mr James O'Farrell. The beautiful front panels of the altars were preserved and put on the walls with metal brackets. This work was undertaken as a gift to the church by Mr Con Creedon, of Whitehall Road.

In November 1996, Fr Des Byrne and his assistant Fr Edmund Purcell came to the end of their term of office in the parish and were replaced by Fr Daithí Kenneally and Fr Colm Earley respectively. With the new housing that has been erected on Kimmage grounds there has been a substantial increase in the number of parishioners. In 1999 Fr Paddy Galvin, who had a wide variety of experience especially in the areas of counselling, spiritual direction and group dynamics, was appointed as Assistant Priest. He was an extremely skilled pastor with a great knowledge of and affection for the people of the parish. During Fr Daithí's tenure the church was completely re-painted, both inside and outside. Our Lady's transept in the church was converted into a beautiful Chapel of Remembrance and when it was completed in August 2000 the names of several hundred deceased Spiritans were already in place on specially prepared slabs on the walls. The ongoing involvement of the parishioners in the life of the parish continued to develop.

Fr Brendan Carr became pastor in 2000. He and Fr Galvin reflected on a pastoral plan for the parish and decided there was need for a listening exercise to hear the needs and preoccupations of the parishioners. They organised the first Parish Assembly in 2001 facilitated by Ms Eilish O'Malley from the Diocesan Development Office. Plans were made to create the first Pastoral Council to respond to the pastoral needs of the community. Its first chairperson was Mr Donal Donovan, who continued that service until 2007, when he handed over to Mrs Catherine O'Malley.

The Pastoral Council undertook visitation of every house in the parish and created committees for liturgy, youth, sacraments, funeral ministry, finance and social activity. With the help of the Pastoral Council, Fr Carr initiated plans to create greater space through converting the large seminary sacristy and surrounding assembly area into a very badly needed parish hall.

Parish offices were transferred from the parochial house on Rockfield Avenue to what used to be the administration offices for the house of studies. These offices are easily accessible to the parishioners and give the excellent parish secretary, Marion Connolly, facilities and space for a proper working environment.

The parish community along with Spiritan community was shocked when Fr Paddy Galvin died in March 2003. A genuine outpouring of grief brought unprecedented numbers to attend his waking and funeral at the parish church. After Fr Galvin's death, Fr Leo Horkin, at eighty-five years of age, agreed to come and serve as curate and gave marvellous consistency of service while he was there.

Fr Jonathan Murray, who was preparing to go on mission to Pakistan, gave almost a year of service to the parish in 2003, bringing a lot of creativity to the liturgy and youth group. Fr Austin Healy, a veteran missionary from Sierra Leone and Ghana, offered his services when Fr Murray left for Pakistan and remained on as curate until he himself left for Tanzania in the autumn of 2010.

In January 2007, Fr Pat Doody took over as Pastor and continued the good work that had been begun. The parish community continued to grow and car spaces were at a premium. The existing car park was expanded to provide fifty extra spaces. The parish offices were renovated around the same time. In July 2010 the church was closed for two weeks to allow a major restoration of the beautiful parquet floors to what they would have looked like in October 1938 when the chapel was blessed. A similar project of restoration for the sacristy and parish hall floors took place in July 2011. A webcam system was installed in the church in April 2011 so that anyone with an internet facility can view all the liturgical celebrations live anywhere in the world.

At the heart of Kimmage parish life is the Sunday Eucharist. Of special importance is the family Mass at 10.00 a.m. every Sunday. This had its origins way back when Spiritan students gave their time each Sunday to pastoral work in the church. It has grown and strengthened with the committed group of parents who prepare liturgy with special attention to children and where there is catechesis apart during the Liturgy of the Word for the little ones. The 11.30 a.m. Mass is no less creative where the music group and choir nourish the liturgy all the year round with a beauty and sensitivity that gives life to a vibrant worshipping community.[1]

---

1. Memos from Fr Kennelly, Fr Carr and Fr Doody

CHAPTER SIXTEEN

Marian House

When the Mission House opened in 1958 it was primarily intended as a residence for missionaries on leave, not as a house for retired missionaries. By and large missionaries did not return to Ireland to retire but usually lived out their days in the country where they served long after they had passed 'retirement' age.

A number of factors contributed towards changing this situation. The vast increase in the numbers being trained and sent on the missions eventually led to increasing numbers on the missions who reached 'retirement' age and, of course, larger numbers who incurred illness. Many mission territories were not able to cope with this new situation. More rapid growth of the local churches and an increase in the number of clergy in the new churches led eventually to the local churches taking full responsibility for their own affairs. Missionaries rapidly became redundant in many mission territories and consequently could not be expected to live out their days in the countries where they worked, especially as the number of Spiritan communities and parishes decreased. As well as that a new pattern of mission developed which meant that missionaries moved around a good deal more from one country to another, meaning in turn that they did not put down roots in any one country as they had tended to do in earlier times. Upheavals like the Biafran War created a situation where many Spiritans would have to provide for themselves on retiring or would have to avail of facilities back in Ireland. This was the case with personnel who worked in dioceses in the USA or Britain. From about 1960 onwards Irish Spiritans working in particular countries needed visas and/or work permits, and in some countries these were no longer given or might not be renewed.

By 1980 there were about thirty Spiritans in the Mission House who were sick or retired. While the Mission House provided very fine amenities for active personnel, these amenities did not come up to the standard required for the retired and the sick.

The same kind of problem was being experienced by other missionary and religious congregations. The Conference of Major Religious Superiors (CMRS) had fruitful discussions on the issue during the first half of 1979 which led to the setting up of a Working Party to produce models of a nursing home dependency unit with parameters of capital and current expenditure. Fr Michael McCarthy represented the Spiritans on this Working Party which was to produce a report by 15 August 1979.

In the meantime, a team from the Generalate in Rome came on visitation to the Irish Province. At the Spiritan Provincial Assembly in Blackrock in April 1979, Fr John G. Walsh from the General Council addressed the subject of retired and sick confrères as follows: 'While the Irish Province has done much for its retired confrères there is no doubt that much more will have to be done to plan for the future, since the number of retired confrères will soon greatly increase. Care should be taken to provide houses and surroundings for our aged confrères which are sufficiently comfortable and psychologically helpful. Buildings should be adapted for the purpose, if necessary, and the services of geriatric and medical personnel should be available.[1] With due regard to poverty we think the most comfortable houses in the Province should be those of our retired confrères.' By July, 1979, the Provincial Council was already thinking of having its own nursing unit without waiting for the report from the CMRS.

In September 1979, Fr Jim Shanley and Fr Mick Reynolds took over as superior and bursar respectively in Kimmage. At that time there were three very ill Spiritans in different nursing homes at three different locations in Dublin. Fr Shanley and Fr Reynolds decided it was wrong that these should be cared for outside of a Spiritan community, and therefore initiated discussion to find ways and means of providing for them within the community. Each year at Christmas they wrote to all Irish Spiritans working in the USA, Britain and elsewhere, and those gainfully employed outside of the colleges in Ireland. In their letters they put before the confrères the need to provide for retirement with the 'subtle' suggestion that if any of them had any

---

1. *Guidelines*, 97-102

spare money or met with any generous people who wanted to help the cause, then that money could be sent to Kimmage. The response was immediate, and substantial sums of money were sent by the confrères for the retirement project. Fr Shanley also began to organise raffles, concerts and other fund-raising events.

Through 1980 and 1981 the discussion on the need to provide for the retired and sick confrères continued. It was by no means agreed that the obvious solution was to build a nursing home. There were still many Spiritans who favoured the idea of the sick being sent out to private nursing homes. Others believed that each community should look after its own sick in whatever way it thought best, while some believed that a nursing home for the Province built in Kimmage would be the best solution.

At the Provincial Chapter of June-July 1982, the delegates were convinced that existing facilities and services for retirement would prove inadequate in the years ahead. The new Provincial Administration was mandated to take the necessary action to deal with the matter. As well as that, one of the councillors was to have special responsibility for retirement within the Province and he would advise the Provincial Administration on the provision of a nursing unit and its location and see to the provision of other houses of retirement.

A commission set up to deal with retirement offered two solutions: one was to build a nursing unit, the other was to purchase houses for the active retired. Only the first solution was acted on.[2]

During 1984-85, Fr Shanley and Fr Reynolds employed an architect to draw up plans for a nursing home in Kimmage. When the Provincial Administration heard this they decided to step in and take it over as a Provincial project. Fr Michael McCarthy, the Provincial, employed the services of the firm of architects, Mitchell O'Muire Smyth, to draw up new plans, while the former plans were dropped. Fr Shanley and Fr Reynolds left office in July 1985, but before doing so they handed over to the Provincialate £700,000 which they had collected for the proposed nursing unit.[3]

2. Provincial Chapter 1982, Retirement
3. Michael Reynolds, Notes

The new superior was Fr Michael Duggan, while the new bursar was Fr Michael Buckley. On 13 February 1986, the new plans were submitted to the Provincial and to Kimmage. Much discussion on the details ensued during the following months. Planning permission had already been applied for in January and was granted towards the end of February 1986. Technical and general specifications were finally submitted in August 1986, which enabled the proposed building to be put for tender. The tender of W. & J. Bolger was accepted.

The first sod was cut and the site blessed by Archbishop Thomas Brosnahan, the retired Archbishop of Freetown and Bo, Sierra Leone, on 8 December 1986, in the presence of the Kimmage community. Shortly afterwards work on the building began and continued through 1987 and into the early part of 1988. The new nursing unit, known as 'Marian House', was opened and blessed on 11 February 1988.

The new building was a single-storey, concrete-framed building with block 'infill' walls, with concrete floors throughout finished with carpet and vinyl-tiled floor-coverings. There were two wings which radiated from a spacious circular foyer. These wings contained, in all, seventeen residential units with facilities for toilets and showers designed for people using wheelchairs. There was a low-pitched tiled roof incorporating a number of skylights which created a great sense of brightness within the building even on dull days. Off the foyer there was an oratory, matron's office, two reception rooms for visitors, a residents' common room, a reception desk and a kitchen.

Within three years of being opened, it was realised that these facilities were inadequate. A Nursing Care Committee was established by the Provincial Council on 12 November 1991. The committee members were Fr Brendan Hally, Fr Tom O'Malley and Fr Mick Reynolds. By April 1992, they had presented their report and recommendations for the extension of nursing care facilities within the Province. The report was based on visits to nursing units of eight religious orders and congregations, discussions with the matron and staff of Marian House, the Kimmage community, other Irish communities and interested individuals. An architect, Mr Stephen Tierney of Stephen Tierney and Associates, was engaged to make drawings of possible extensions and/or adaptations to the Mission House and Marian House in Kimmage. Four of these drawings were presented to the Provincial Council. In general outline, the plan accepted was similar to what was finally constructed. This initial plan went through many modifications after discussions with all concerned, especially with the matron, Mary Hurley, and the staff of Marian House. The matron's constructive suggestions were most helpful. Some deficiencies which were found to exist in the original plan were rectified. The extension was for a twelve-bed unit joined to the existing building by means of three link corridors. The matron's office and treatment room, and the physiotherapy room were separated from the bedrooms. A bright new dining room and much needed storage space were also provided.

The builders were Bradco Contractors Ltd, Dunshaughlin, who completed the extension by October 1993. It was blessed and formally opened by Fr Brian McLaughlin at a ceremony held in the nursing unit that month. The new extension was called St Bernadette's, but the whole building is usually referred to as Marian House.

Along with the mission house, Marian House is one of the finest assets of the Province, providing as it does a fine facility for sick and invalided confrères. Much gratitude is due to those who had the wisdom, foresight and perseverance to go through with it.

The capital expenditure on the original Marian House came to over one million pounds, while the extension cost nearly three-quarters of a million. The funds came from a wide variety of sources. As stated, Fr Shanley and Fr Reynolds raised most of the money for the original building. Money also came from promotions teams in Ireland and America. Fr Jim Delaney raised funds through Foundations in the USA. Other sources of funding were the past pupils of Spiritan Colleges, the other Irish Spiritan communities who contributed generously, and the Spiritans working in dioceses in Ireland, England and the USA.

Since its foundation Marian House has performed an inestimable service to the community and Province. It has been served by an extraordinarily dedicated nursing staff, nurse assistants, cleaning and maintenance staff. Many members of staff have served in Marian House since it first opened. Mary Hurley, who became the first matron in 1988, still serves as matron for the clinic now in the Mission House. Since November 2000, Regina Sheridan has been matron.

But in the business of health care Dr Desmond Coady holds the record. He has been Medical Officer for Kimmage since 1971 in succession to Dr Ivor Hooper. Dr Coady has given forty years of most dedicated service not just to the residents of Marian House but to the whole Kimmage community including the students in their time, the active members, the retired and missionaries on leave. During that period of time he has got to know all the members of the Province along with their ailments. He is not just a medical doctor. He has become a confidant to many and has a marvellous sense of humour and the gifts of empathy and compassion which enables him to cheer up the most despondent soul.

Epilogue

The story of Kimmage is a story of change, not just in the Spiritan period, but in all the previous centuries. It is a good illustration of what the sixth-century Greek philosopher, Heraclitus, taught: nothing is permanent except change. All change is a kind of death; we always lose something, and perhaps we gain something. Just as grief is necessary to cope with death and to enable the mourners to return to normality, so also grief is necessary to cope with change. Many are saddened that the old formation house has gone, the beautiful grounds, but above all the large numbers of students who once gave immense life to Kimmage. There are many ways of coping with the past that is gone, and with the new things that are emerging. We can refuse to accept that the past is gone. The pathetic literary example of those who cannot accept change is Miss Havisham, the deserted bride in Charles Dickens's *Great Expectations*: she sat for years in her faded wedding gown surrounded by the ruins of her wedding reception; all the clocks in the house had been stopped at 'twenty minutes to nine'. The alternative is to be open to the Spirit, like the old man Simeon in St Luke's gospel, who was prepared to accept the newness of God even if it appeared in a small, frail baby wrapped from head to foot in baby clothes. We are now being challenged, as our predecessors were, to arrange space in our lives for the new to emerge and be received.

BIBLIOGRAPHY

IRISH PROVINCIAL ARCHIVES

Bulletin Général de la Congregation
Bulletin of the Province of Ireland
Constitutions. *Regulae et Constitutiones Congregationis Sancti Spiritus.*
(1956 revision)
General Chapter 1968-1969. Directives and Decisions
General Customary of the Congregation. Mother House, Paris 1959
Mission (Student review of Mission in 1970s)
Provincial Chapter of Ireland 1970. Congregation of the Holy Ghost
Spectrum (Magazine of the House of Theology 1960s-1980s)
Spiritan Rule of Life. Congregation of the Holy Spirit, 1987
Tomorrow's Labourers (Annual review of House of Philosophy)

ARCHIVES OF BLACKROCK COLLEGE

Fr Martin Ebenrecht's Journal of Blackrock College

UNPUBLISHED ARTICLES

Quinn, Richard   *The Development Studies Centre 1978-1998.* (1998)
Raftery, Thomas   *Father Hugh Murray Gunn Evans,* C.S.Sp. (1860-
                   1943). (2011)
Reilly, Paddy   *Brief History of Kimmage DSC and Holy Ghost
                   College.* (2011)
Whelan, Thomas   *The Kimmage Mission Institute
                   Serving Theology. The Kimmage Mission Institute.*

MEMOIRS, MEMOS AND NOTES

Carr, Brendan C.S.Sp.
Crowley, Timothy C.S.Sp.
Curran, Roddy C.S.Sp.
Doody, Patrick C.S.Sp.
Dowling, Oliver (James) C.S.Sp.
Grimes, Edward C.S.Sp.
Heeran, Pádraig
Kane, Michael C.S.Sp.
Kelly, Martin A. C.S.Sp.
Lynch, Philip C.S.Sp.

McLaughlin, Brian C.S.Sp.
Reynolds, Michael C.S.Sp.
Roche, Thomas C.S.Sp.
Ryan, Edmund C. S.Sp.

INTERVIEWS AND INFORMAL CONVERSATIONS
Chisholm, John C.S.Sp.
Darcy, Stephen C.S.Sp.
Duggan, James C.S.Sp.
Dundon, Patrick C.S.Sp.
Foley, Gerard C.S.Sp.
Geoghegan, Anthony C.S.Sp.
Martin, Liam C.S.Sp.
Meagher, Thomas F. C.S.Sp.
Nugent, William C.S.Sp.
Shanley, Ciarán C.S.Sp.

PRINTED WORKS
Bokenkotter, Thomas   *A Concise History of the Catholic Church.*
                        (revised and expanded edition 1990)
Burke, Christy   *No Longer Slaves: The Mission of Francis*
                        Libermann (1802-1852). (2010)
Burke's Peerage
Byrne, Joseph et al.   *A Review of the History and Development*
                        of the Irish Province of the Congregation of
                        the Holy Ghost and the Immaculate Heart
                        of Mary, 1859-1924.
Byrne, Tony   *Airlift to Biafra. Breaching the Blockade.* (1997)
Carty, Francis Xavier   *Why I Said No To God.* (1986)
Duffy, Eamon   *Saints and Sinners. A History of the Popes.*
                        (3rd edition 2006)
Farragher, Seán P.   *Bishop Shanahan C.S.Sp. Selected Studies.*
Farragher, Seán P.   *Blackrock College 1860-1995.*
Farragher, Seán P.   *Irish Spiritans Remembered.*
Farragher, Seán P.   *Père Leman, Educator and Missionary 1826-*
                        1880.
Fay, Myles   'Finances', *Go Teach all Nations*, ed. Enda
                        Watters. (2000)

Ferriter, Diarmaid   *The Transformation of Ireland 1900-2000.*
                            (2005)
Geoghegan, Anthony   'Formation', *Go Teach all Nations*, ed. Enda
                            Watters. (2000)
Geoghegan, Anthony   'Apostolic Life' *Spiritan Horizons*, issue 3, Fall
                            2008.
Hogan, Edmund M.   *The Irish Missionary Movement. A Historical
                            Survey, 1830-1980.* (1990)
Kennedy, Denis   *Memories of the Biafran War.*
Keogh, Dermot   *Twentieth Century Ireland.* (1994)
Kilkenny, Michael   'A Merger, An Attempted Takeover … Turning
                            points in the Spiritan Story' *Spiritan Horizons*,
                            issue 5, Fall 2010.
Koren, Henry J.   *The Spiritans. A history of the Congregation of
                            the Holy Ghost.*
Little, Seán   'Our Chapel', *Tomorrows' Labourers* 1953.
Maher, William A.   *A History of St Mary's College Rathmines,
                            Dublin 1890-1990.*
O'Hanrahan, Jack   'Flight from Louvain', Rockwell Annual.
                            (1941)
O'Reilly, Hugh   'The Old House', *Tomorrow's Labourers* 1954
Watters, Enda (ed.)   *Go Teach All Nations. A History of the Irish
                            Province of the Congregation of the Holy Spirit.*
                            (2000)

INDEX